365 DAYS OF
Self-Care
FOR
New
Mums

Advice for Surviving (and Thriving) in Baby's First Year

ZEENA
MOOLLA

An Hachette UK Company
www.hachette.co.uk

Vie Books, an imprint of Summersdale Publishers
Part of Octopus Publishing Group Limited
Carmelite House
50 Victoria Embankment
LONDON
EC4Y 0DZ
UK

www.summersdale.com

The authorized representative in the EEA is Hachette Ireland, 8 Castlecourt Centre, Dublin 15, D15 XTP3, Ireland (email: info@hbgi.ie)

Printed and bound in Poland

ISBN: 978-1-80007-673-0

This FSC® label means that materials used for the product have been responsibly sourced

MIX
Paper | Supporting responsible forestry
FSC® C018236

Substantial discounts on bulk quantities of Summersdale books are available to corporations, professional associations and other organizations. For details contact general enquiries: telephone: +44 (0) 1243 771107 or email: enquiries@summersdale.com.

CONTENTS

Introduction

Welcome to motherhood! HUGE congratulations on your gorgeous, brand-new baby.

How's it going? Exactly the way it's depicted – a serene, unbelievably fresh-faced mum holding aloft a beautiful baby bearing a gummy grin of cartoon-cute proportions – on the cover of a baby magazine? Or does motherhood more closely resemble a crime scene, thanks to a little sleep thief turning your life upside down and leaving a devastation of baby-related debris in its wake? If you lean more to the latter, you're far from alone.

There's no doubt about it, motherhood is like nothing else. The undying devotion you feel for your baby is staggeringly strong. But the first twelve months of a baby's life can be such an emotional rollercoaster for many new mums. You might spend much of it veering between love and lunacy, wondering how this tiny, adorable human could possibly be responsible for so much chaos. And that's a totally typical experience for the first year of motherhood. While taking care of your baby is priority, you mustn't lose sight of the other primary person in this situation: *you*. This book, packed with 365 tips and self-care quotes, is your new best friend, here to hold your hand every day. Because in order to be the best possible mother you can be to your beautiful new baby, you need to look after yourself, too.

WEEK ONE

01

Roll with it

To say life with a newborn is unpredictable is like describing a hurricane as a bit breezy. The sooner you can surrender to the situation, the easier it'll be. It's not an easy mindset to adopt when you're pacing the floor at 3 a.m., wondering how such a tiny sweet thing can be so unreasonable, but for these first few weeks, just try to concentrate on the here and now.

02

Veto the visitors

If you're struggling to follow your own train of thought, let alone a conversation about the traffic, veto the visitors because being "on form" is not a priority right now.

**Breastfeeding should not be taboo, and
bottle feeding should not be judged.
It's ALL fun for the whole family.**

JAIME KING

Fed is best

For many new mums, it can often feel like everyone's main concern is with how baby is fed, with the mother's perspective and needs vastly, and dangerously, overlooked. If you're feeling pressured or "spoken over" with regard to how you feed your baby, be it bottle or breast, some boundaries need to be set. Practise, if need be, holding your nerve by smiling and saying out loud: "*I'll* work out what's best for my baby." You can be as breezy or as firm as you like, but in order to be the best possible mother you can be to your baby, you must make your voice heard. You're the one in the driving seat; everyone, including yourself, needs to be clear on this.

Postnatal body

You've just grown a human and unsurprisingly, your body is making known the enormity of this in various ways, including uterus cramping, bleeding and discharge. This is all perfectly normal and a sign your body is doing what it needs to do. Stock up on thick maternity pads, and ask your midwife (or doctor) about pain relief for any cramp pain.

C-section care

If you gave birth via Caesarean section (C-section), make sure you gently clean and pat dry your incision with soap and water once a day. Talk to your doctor or midwife about whether it's better to cover the wound or leave it open to air out. Most importantly, avoid carrying most things (besides your baby). And, should this not be apparent, hold off on exercising until your midwife or doctor confirms it's OK to do so.

For three months, I was walking around
my house with a top knot and giant diaper
– like a defeated sumo wrestler...

ALI WONG

No cooking!

Even if your idea of cooking is typically slinging some bread in a toaster and resentfully opening a tin of beans, now is *not* the time to be preparing meals. Let your partner, friend, family member, anyone but you, assume that role. Encourage visitors to bring nourishing freezer food (curries, casseroles, soups, etc.). Pull out all the takeaway menus rammed in the kitchen drawer. Cooking for these first few weeks should not be a new-mum obligation.

No cleaning!

Stop! Step away from that cloth. Cleaning is not your responsibility either. Make peace with your current situation, even if your house closely resembles a landfill, accepting that a tidy home is a thing of the future; or else, make housework the onus of partners, friends, relatives, visitors – just not you.

You come into our house and a giant elephant and lion are welcoming you. We have toys and things everywhere.

HEIDI KLUM

(11)

Cry baby

"All babies cry." If ever there was a well-worn phrase designed to make a new mum lob tubs of nappy cream at a wall in exasperation, then this might be it. It's never less helpful to hear than when you're in the throes of a particularly shrill and implacable meltdown. Persistent crying – irrespective of whether baby is hungry, tired, has a wet nappy, needs burping – is very common, but this doesn't mean that you have to cope alone. If the crying doesn't stop and you've tried every trick in the book, then take time out by sharing the load with a partner, relative or friend. Speak to your doctor or midwife if you're concerned. Just know that you're not failing as a mother because you can't stop the tears. If help is out there for the taking, take it.

(12)

Breast friend

Make lanolin cream your best friend, applying it liberally to your nipples and areolas after each feed, or if your breasts are feeling particularly sore, as and when it's needed.

13

Navigating guilt trips

A new-mum survey commissioned by *Time* magazine in the US found that 70 per cent of its participants admitted to experiencing guilt in some form. From breastfeeding and bottle feeding to "natural births" and drug-assisted ones, early motherhood can be fraught with pressure – and therefore, sadly, self-shame. While it can be a difficult emotion to simply switch off, it's crucial not to let guilt become a dominant feature in your life.

If such feelings are starting to preoccupy you, a simple exercise to tackle this is to practise a little mindfulness: acknowledge your guilt, identify its source and, as you explore it, consciously replace negative, reproachful inner dialogue with self-compassion. It's not about suppressing guilt, but rather about not letting it spiral – navigating it consciously while being kind to yourself. Most importantly, remind yourself (daily if need be) that a good parent is simply a loving one.

14

Motherhood is a struggle of a little more time there, a little more time here, and feeling a little bit guilty all the time.

HALLE BERRY

Snap happy

Mother Nature is not stupid, is she? She designed babies so cute, they have the ability to wipe clean memories of sleep deprivation and nerve-shattering meltdowns (hence why people often go on to have more than one baby!). In those rare moments of quiet (perhaps during a feed or nap), squeeze in a quick photo or three; as any new mum will tell you, you'll never regret taking an inordinate amount of pictures during these magical, mayhem-filled weeks.

I want to *sleeep!*

Whoever coined that phrase "sleep like a baby" was clearly not the parent of a newborn because there's no sugar-coating it, looking after a newborn often feels pretty sleep-averse. But sleep will come; remind yourself of this regularly, without fixating on when and how.

(17)

Power nap

If pre-motherhood sleep feels like a nostalgic distant memory, you'll be pleased to hear that napping has been proven by multiple studies to have numerous health benefits. Just 20 minutes of daytime sleep is apparently enough to turn off your nervous system, recharge your whole body and vastly improve your cognitive function (including short-term memory and reaction time). If power napping doesn't come naturally to you, then don't stress, there are other ways to recharge your batteries (see next tip).

(18)

No guilt zzzone

New mums are often advised to try and sleep the minute baby hits the crib. It's sensible advice of course (as detailed above), but it's often easier said than done, especially if this is the only opportunity to shower, eat or enjoy a tea without it turning stone cold. So don't let the "sleep while baby sleeps" adage become a source of guilt. Eating, bathing, sipping tea, enjoying a little Netflix – these are all vital forms of rejuvenation, too.

Nobody talks about the first six weeks after you have the baby. What a rollercoaster! [But] it's the best decision I've ever made in my entire life.

KATY PERRY

First post-labour poo!

Many new mums experience constipation after giving birth for a variety of reasons: from milk production disrupting your system to anxiety over that first poo (especially true for mums who've had stitches for an episiotomy or tear during delivery). To help ease constipation, drink plenty of water and try to eat fibre-rich foods. If four days pass without a bowel movement after giving birth, speak to your doctor about a stool softener.

Baby blues

Do not underestimate the power of those postnatal hormones. A new-mum survey in the US found that 80 per cent of participants experienced the "baby blues", a mild form of postnatal depression (PND), also known as postpartum depression (PPD). The condition occurs almost immediately after giving birth, often lasting for around two weeks. Again, don't suffer in silence, but talk it through with a healthcare professional. Remember you are not alone; this *will* pass.

Maternal instinct myth

Were your first thoughts when they discharged you and your baby from hospital less of elation but more of horror at the thought that you were expected to raise a child unsupervised, without some sort of manual for reference? "Maternal instinct" can become a form of pressure for new mums, with notions of motherhood as something innate widely touted in society. You will undoubtedly develop a gut instinct about your child. Some things will come naturally, other stuff, you'll learn. Motherhood is often fraught with self-doubt, but never take this to mean you don't have a connection with your child, or worse, view it as a barometer for the kind of mum you are.

I have to keep reminding myself that I am their mother. Sometimes we are sitting at home and I feel like we are waiting for our mum to come home.

RUBY WAX

**It takes a village, and it's really hard
to be the village on your own.**

SELMA BLAIR

I need help!

Getting help isn't a sign of weakness, it's a sign of strength. When you're struggling to carry the load single-handedly or you've lost balance in your life, summoning the courage to admit this to yourself and others is an act of real love – for both you and your baby. Talk to someone (whether that's to a relative, friend, colleague, professional – whoever you prefer) if you're feeling overwhelmed by things. Just don't suffer in silence and, where possible, enlist some assistance with your load. The lovely African proverb, "It takes a village to raise a child" (meaning, parenting is a shared responsibility) is so true, and you might be surprised by just how many people share this view.

Ask away

As a new mother, it is totally reasonable to have a head filled with questions. Never worry about leaning on your midwife or health visitor if you're unsure of anything. It's what they're there for!

You're a fab mum

There will likely be days when climbing under a duvet and setting up a nice studio apartment there is tempting; days when you're so tired, you find yourself envying the cat's luxury to sleep at will; days when nipping to the corner shop for a pint of semi-skimmed feels about as feasible as nipping to the Bahamas for a fortnight; days when you even find yourself resentful of motherhood. None of this makes you a bad mother because – newsflash – you're human. And a pretty excellent one at that for doing your utmost for the sake of your child. As you begin your new life as a mother, *always* remember this.

(28)

You make it work. You keep getting out of bed. Sometimes it's just because you know there's a cup of coffee downstairs.

MICHELLE WILLIAMS

(29)

Tired tales to tickle!

If the sleep deprivation is hitting hard now, then seek out other new mums, even if only over WhatsApp or by text, and swap some sleepless tales to turn things around. The mum so tired she was about to fetch her baby from his crib only to realize she was already nursing him? The woman who hurriedly climbed into the shower forgetting to remove both her clothes and glasses first? The new mother who spent the morning trying to locate her mobile phone, found it in the dryer, then promptly lost it again and subsequently spent the rest of the day hunting once more because she'd inexplicably placed it in the fridge? All true! All funny! All helpful for taking the edge off wretched restless nights.

WEEK TWO

30

Drink in that baby!

Look at that little nose! Those cute tiny toes! And that teeny tight grip of your forefinger is just heart melting. It's pretty amazing, isn't it? That a group of cells developed inside a womb to create this adorable human being now in your life. Enjoy drinking this in. It's real life-affirming stuff.

31

Wash carefully

Avoid washing with anything but plain water if you have perineal stitches (soap might irritate an already tender area). Gently pat dry, changing maternity pads when full. For extra comfort, wear loose cotton knickers or dare to go commando (the air will hasten the healing process)!

Ice, ice baby

If it feels particularly sore or itchy in the perineal area, ice can really help to soothe the discomfort: very gently apply an ice pack or cold compress, every hour if you can, to reduce swelling and subsequent irritation.

New-parent rows

If you're raising your baby with a partner and suddenly find yourselves bickering or rowing a lot, perhaps even turning the air blue with some very choice words, then you're far from alone. Research shows that couples argue 40 per cent more after having a baby, and the newborn weeks are the most testing. Go easy on yourselves and don't base your relationship's future on a barbed remark or late-night row. You're two new parents just trying your best to look after a baby on ridiculously low levels of sleep. Things *will* get tetchy on occasion. In fact, with nine out of ten new parents admitting to rowing more often, it would be more surprising if you didn't!

It's not just all diapers and blankets and hair-bows. We have to open our hearts and realize there are going to be hard moments, too.

HILARIA BALDWIN

Fresh air self-care

Being cooped up with your baby for any length of time can leave you feeling like you're living on Planet Parent while the outside world feels like a galaxy far, far away. A lack of energy and time during these all-consuming newborn weeks can see a new mum yearning for daylight and air that doesn't smell like a fusty attic. Getting outside, as we know, is vital for our physical health. But it's not just a decent dose of bone-strengthening vitamin D we stand to benefit from. Studies indicate that around 20 to 30 minutes of sunlight exposure in all weathers can significantly boost serotonin levels and thereafter your emotional wellbeing. So if cabin fever is setting in, make an effort to venture out, even if only for a bask on the doorstep or cup of tea in the back garden.

Short walks

Right now, with your body in postnatal recovery, it's probably not a good idea to go overexerting yourself. However, while rest is essential, your body will benefit from *some* movement, so when you can, go for short walks to lubricate your stiff joints and get your circulation moving.

Let's talk about sex, baby!

It's likely that sex is the farthest thing from your mind right now, but in terms of when it's safe to do so, you should allow your body time to fully recover. If you have stitches, it could take at least a couple of months for these to heal and ideally, you should wait until the post-birth bleeding stops. Remember too, that unless you're planning to get pregnant, breastfeeding is not a reliable form of contraception, so be careful!

Pelvic floor exercises

An activity you can start doing almost immediately after giving birth (as long as you don't have a catheter in place) is pelvic floor (or Kegel) exercise. Do this by gently clenching your pelvic muscles (preferably while in a standing position), holding for about 10 seconds, and then releasing. Repeat several times, two to three times a day if you can. Should you experience any pain as you attempt this, then wait until you're feeling stronger before trying again.

When you have a baby, you go through a period where your body is not your own. It becomes for your child.

CHRISTINA AGUILERA

I am completely changed since being a mom. I'm much more open, I'm much more accepting of myself, I'm much more thoughtful.

PINK

You've changed

Maybe you vowed before becoming a mum that motherhood wouldn't change you. But there's no shame in admitting it has. Many new mums report feeling like the world is entirely different the minute they step outside hospital. Some mums say they discover a fiercely protective side of their personality that didn't feature pre-baby, while others describe a serenity they'd not experienced before. In whatever way motherhood changes you, embrace it. You're still you. Your identity is just evolving and you shouldn't feel obliged to deny having a new perspective on life while you're going through a pretty all-consuming experience – especially if this obligation is motivated by some form of societal pressure. Say it loud, say it proud: "I am a mum!"

Bit windy!

Hormones can take their toll on a new mum's bowel movements, often leading to excess gas – especially true if you gave birth via C-section (your intestines can be slower moving afterwards). If you're more gassy than normal, try sipping more water, upping your fibre intake and doing some gentle walking. It will pass (pardon the pun). In the meantime, try not to worry if a little wind escapes while you're in company (just blame the dog, your partner, your baby even!).

Peed yourself laughing?

Sneezing, laughing, running for a bus – ask most mothers how their relationship with these things changed post birth, and you'll be greeted with a wry smile. It's hugely common for a new mum to experience urinary incontinence after having a baby, and often simple things like bursting into laughter or breaking into a sprint can cause a little bladder leakage. Symptoms should improve within a few months, but if you've any concerns, speak to your midwife (or doctor).

Mother's milk

Drinking a cup of milk before bed may sound like the sort of advice a more mature relative would dish out, but there's scientific evidence to suggest that doing just that could improve quality of sleep. Equally, soya is rich in tryptophan (an amino acid with sedative effects). For extra comfort, warm your milk first (apparently, warm beverages are more soothing than cold ones).

Don't dare diet

Own a set of bathroom scales? Shove them in the loft or at the back of the cupboard. Now is *not* the time to preoccupy yourself with weight loss. A new mum burns on average 7,000 calories during labour, 500 a day breastfeeding and 100 an hour carrying a newborn around. Even sleep deprivation depletes your energy reserves. If anything, you need extra energy!

I've been on a diet my whole life. But once I gave birth, I didn't want to think about myself or feel insecure about my career; I wanted to think about my child. So I stopped worrying about diets.

LIV TYLER

News-stand pressure

When you're passing a news-stand in the supermarket and see reams of magazine covers blasting out baby weight loss plans and the diet secrets of celebrity new mums, look away – they're not your friends. Rather, these magazines prey on a new mum's insecurity by creating unhelpful pressure to conform to an unrealistic physique that looks as if nothing as momentously life- or body-changing as having a baby has occurred. See these mags as mere rags and move on. You have a body that was able to carry and birth life – that's a healthy, phenomenal, beautiful body.

Swerve supplements

Similarly, give the diet supplement sections of the supermarket, health food store and internet a swerve. Aside from the apparent lack of scientific evidence proving their efficacy, diet supplements can contain ingredients above the recommended dose, which can be particularly dangerous in breastfeeding mums. Eat well, sleep (when you can) and enjoy your baby; that's all that matters right now.

C sense

Recovery from a **C**-section birth is typically slower than that of vaginal birth. The likelihood is that you'll feel a little sore for a few weeks. If other **C**-section mums appear to be healing quicker than you, remember it's futile to compare yourself. Every labour is unique and your recovery will progress at your body's natural speed. And do take your painkillers as prescribed (even on the days when you don't think they're necessary, they will be helping with inflammation).

C-section soothing

C-section mothers will likely be advised to remove their dressing after 24 hours to let their wound air. As the wound begins to heal and the stitches dissolve (roughly within a week), the area can become a little itchy. However tempting, it's really important that you don't scratch it. Instead, soothe the irritability by very gently applying some aftersun to the area. Try an ice-pack if that fails.

(51)

Support your back

It stands to reason that if you grow and carry a baby for nine months, you're going to have symptoms of a bad back. Any back pain you may be experiencing is likely to fade, but there are ways to aid recovery. Whichever way you feed your baby, remember to support your back sufficiently with cushions and by adopting a relaxed seated position. Try to get into the habit of changing your baby's nappy in a comfortable standing position rather than on the floor, too. And where possible, enlist regular help to lift and carry your baby. Your core muscles will have taken a big hit during pregnancy and you won't be as strong in the trunk as you were pre-baby. Pay attention to your sites of pain and act accordingly. If the pain you're experiencing is extreme, speak to a medical professional and maybe try postnatal physiotherapy.

(52)

I believe in a world where mothers are not expected to shed any physical evidence of their child-bearing experience.

OLIVIA WILDE

Embrace body changes

A few body changes can occur during pregnancy, changes you might just have to accept. For many new mums, it's wider ribs and hips, for others, it's darker nipples and areolas. Some even go up in shoe size, which can only mean one thing for those pre-baby shoes: a new home. It's totally normal to have mixed feelings, but try to keep perspective – your body carried out a pretty important purpose and these changes are testimony to that.

Symptoms never to ignore

A high temperature, abdominal pain and foul-smelling discharge are typical signs of a postnatal infection, however you gave birth. Never ignore these; you could be suffering from a urinary tract infection, puerperal mastitis, endometritis (all very common after giving birth). Similarly, if you gave birth via C-section and notice any discharge or a strong smell from your wound, get this looked at immediately. Treatment is typically straightforward and nothing to be scared about, but such matters need to be diagnosed urgently for the correct course of action.

Sleep at this point is just a concept, something I'm looking forward to investigating in the future.

AMY POEHLER

Don't cherish every moment!

"Cherish every moment" is a phrase you might hear a lot, even before baby's arrived. But when you're surviving on 45 minutes' sleep, have sick in your hair and haven't had a chance to dine on much beyond packets of cheese and onion crisps, it's not always easy advice to follow. So don't! Accept how you're feeling. Talk it out with friends or relatives. Don't be ashamed to admit to feeling resentful of motherhood. This'll never make you a bad mum – it makes you a human being.

Mother of lies

News just in: some parents lie! If you're encountering tales of babies sleeping 10 hours straight and adjusting to daytime nap routines like ducks to water, take it with a pinch of salt. One online survey found that almost half of the 11,000 new-parent participants admitted to lying about their baby's sleep schedules. The only feeling you should be entertaining this with is pity, not resentment!

In the sling of it

Baby slings (a piece of fabric specifically designed to let you carry your baby against your torso), can be a brilliant means of keeping your hands free and feeling close to your little one. For your baby, it can resemble being back in the womb as they enjoy hearing your heartbeat, your body's warmth and the rocking sensation as you move about. It can also be a great way to soothe your baby to sleep, or provide comfort when wind, colic or reflux is being particularly bothersome. Plus you can get on with chores, talk on the phone and even enjoy a snack in peace while wearing one!

I wear scarves because if my baby has an accident and I'm holding the baby, I'm not walking around with a big puke stain or poo stain on my shirt!

JESSICA ALBA

WEEK THREE

60

Pee relief

If you have perineal stitches and are finding peeing particularly painful, keep a jug of warm water handy when the need to wee strikes. Pouring water over your vagina and perineum dilutes the acidity of the urine, helping to ease stinging and keep the stitches clean. Afterwards, gently pat your vagina dry to prevent any irritation.

61

Piling on pain

Haemorrhoids are very common post giving birth. Your midwife (or doctor) may prescribe some cream. For instant relief, try using a cooling pad. Most post-pregnancy haemorrhoids clear up by themselves in a few weeks, so they shouldn't be a pain in the butt for long!

Creating a human takes a toll on women's bodies. Sometimes we don't give ourselves enough love or patience about that.

DANIELLE BROOKS

Achy body

Given what your body's gone through, it's likely you'll be feeling pretty sore over the coming weeks. Soothe your aching muscles in a warm bath with Epsom salts for about 20 minutes (every day if you can). If you have dissolvable stitches and/or gave birth via C-section, stick to plain water at least until your midwife (or doctor) says otherwise (the salt can make the stitches dissolve too quickly and aggravate the wound).

All hail dry shampoo!

Unfamiliar with the game-changing merits of dry shampoo? It's about time you got acquainted. Not just great for extending the lifetime of a good blow dry or bringing life to limp locks – it's also the ultimate de-greaser for new mums with barely enough time to undress for a shower, let alone wash their hair! A good dry shampoo can buy several days of unwashed hair and help you feel less like a walking deep fat fryer!

Mastitis treatment

Mastitis is an infection of the mammary gland which can affect both breast and bottle-feeding mums. Hormonal changes and blocked milk ducts are common causes. Symptoms (usually only in one breast) include, among others, a hard, red swelling that feels hot and painful to touch. As any new mum who has experienced this will tell you, mastitis can be miserable, but the sooner you seek medical advice and treatment, the sooner it's likely to disappear (often in a matter of days).

I want to give a big virtual hug to all the mammas out there who have any type of issue breastfeeding. You are not alone.

LAUREN PAUL

Supported is best

For many mums, the decision to stop breastfeeding can be hugely emotional – especially if an issue like mastitis has become too painful to endure. If for whatever reason you choose to stop, let non-judgemental, fact-based information guide your decision. Speak to your midwife (or doctor) for extra resource ideas. Remember, you don't deserve to be shamed or pressured in any way.

Feeding for pain relief

If you've developed mastitis while breastfeeding but wish to continue, the general medical advice is to keep it up as much as possible. Many lactation consultants recommend feeding with the infected breast first, pumping any engorgement (swelling) away in between feeds. You can also try massaging your breast, stroking from the lumpy or sore area towards your nipple, to clear any blockages and aid milk flow.

It's hard. Some of us can't do it. I managed about nine weeks with my boobs.

ADELE

Warm cloth for pain relief

Seeking medical advice is a must if you suspect you have mastitis. You can help to relieve the pain in the meantime by soaking a cloth in warm water and placing it on your breast. Taking ibuprofen and paracetamol can also help to ease the pain. But aspirin should be avoided (unless advised by your doctor) due to adverse effects it's thought to have on breastfed infants.

Matter of opinion

Motherhood, as may already be apparent to you, is awash with unsolicited advice: "I'd put a hat on that baby if I were you." "She's a thumb sucker. You'd better put a stop to that now unless you want a bucktooth baby!" "Have you got that book, *How to Make Your Baby Sleep All Night the Minute You're Home From the Hospital*? Oh, you HAVE to read it!"

No matter how well-intended or thinly veiled it is, uninvited opinion can drive a new mother to distraction. Confrontation in such circumstances is rarely helpful, so try mastering the art of deflection: smile, nod and then change the subject. Remember, your instinct and your child are all that matter.

You innately know what your child needs. You should trust that.

LUCY LIU

Postnatal supplements

For breastfeeding mothers shopping for a good postnatal vitamin, look for a supplement that contains folic acid, iron (anaemia can be common in new mums), vitamin D and calcium. Some postnatal vitamins also contain botanicals like moringa and fenugreek, both of which have been found to aid milk production.

Having a baby is just living in the constant unexpected. You never know when you're gonna get crapped on or when you're gonna get a big smile or when that smile immediately turns to hysterics.

BLAKE LIVELY

Dairy-free mums

Don't eat dairy? You can still get calcium from non-dairy food sources. Tofu is an excellent source and fab for a quick meal with vegetables (broccoli is another great way of getting calcium into your diet) and noodles. Other non-dairy calcium sources include brown bread, pulses and dried fruit. Just eat foods containing high levels of calcium as well as taking a supplement – research indicates that bones are fortified more effectively when calcium is consumed by dietary means.

Tooth truth

If it's taking you until mid-afternoon to realize you haven't brushed your teeth, then you're not alone; this sort of thing is to be expected as you try to establish a routine. The matter of raising a small person quite rightly takes priority, but it's important not to neglect your own needs. Research shows that we should be brushing our teeth first thing, not after breakfast (as many of us do) because the plaque-causing bacteria in your mouth multiplies while you sleep – leaving that furry mouth feeling and ever-so delightful morning breath upon waking; eating breakfast with last night's plaque sitting on your teeth can increase the risk of weakened enamel and cavities. For optimum oral care, aim to leave off eating for at least 30 minutes after brushing.

Teeth-friendly foods

Don't feel too guilty when you're chomping on quick and easy snacks like crackers and breadsticks between feeds; dental research has shown that these sorts of snack food (not the highly processed, cavity-inducing varieties) can actually improve gum health.

(78)

Single-mum mentor

All mothers could probably do with a mum mentor: someone to walk them through motherhood every step of the way, showing them there's light at the end of the tunnel on the tough days and reminding them there's so much to look forward to. This is perhaps especially true for single mums. If you're that person, try to connect with another mother, perhaps a few or more years ahead of you in parenting terms, and speak regularly to this person. If finding another single mum is tricky, speak to a local single-parent charity. Just having someone at the end of the phone can be such a tonic when you're in need of a chat with someone who truly gets it.

(79)

For a moment, it was kind of scary. Like, can I do this by myself? But then that feeling went away, because the reality is, I'm not doing it by myself. I'm surrounded by family and friends who love and support me.

MINDY KALING

Gassy baby

Breastfeeding mums are sometimes advised to avoid eating food that may cause wind or reflux in their babies – food like broccoli, cauliflower and cabbage, plus fruits high in citric acid (such as pineapples and berries). Yet, research suggests that gassy food types in a breastfeeding mum's diet are unlikely to be the root cause of wind or reflux in their baby. More likely accountable is a baby's immature gastrointestinal system. In fact, it's probably more helpful, if reflux in particular is becoming overwhelming, to eliminate both dairy and soya proteins (widely touted as aggravators of symptomatic wind) from your diet. Do, though, get medical advice before removing anything from your diet – as a new mum, a varied nutritious diet is essential for self-care.

Zap those zits

If you're sporting pimples after years of zit-free skin, you can probably put that down to changes in your progesterone levels. But did you know nappy cream can be a really effective spot buster? Just apply directly to the pimple area and leave overnight.

Lactation smoothie

A lactation smoothie contains ingredients believed to help breastfeeding mums stimulate milk production. Despite the unappetizing name, they can be really tasty. Try the recipe below, blitzing all the ingredients into a smooth liquid. Enjoy!

- 4 oz oats
- 4 oz frozen strawberries
- 125 ml milk (any kind)

- 1 banana
- 1 tbsp honey
- 1 tbsp ground flaxseed

I feel sexier after having a baby. I think you feel a lot more confident and much more appreciative of your body and what it's capable of doing.

RACHEL WEISZ

Ginger spice

If you're looking for a really quick and easy galactagogue (any food, herb or spice that boosts milk supply), then consider integrating ginger into your diet; though generally considered safe to eat, it's always worth checking with your midwife (or doctor) first if you have any medical conditions.

**My priorities have changed, and if
I had to choose between having my
roots touched up and hanging out with
my son, I'd always choose him.**

LARA STONE

Eating little and often

Snacking often is the only thing a relentless feeding-on-demand schedule will permit during these early weeks. Eating in this way can be beneficial, though, preventing blood sugar levels from dipping and exacerbating mood swings. This doesn't mean snacking on family-size chocolate bars (that would have the opposite effect!). Rather, it means grazing on nutritious (yet delicious) sustenance like oat crackers with cheese or wholemeal toast topped with banana.

Milk drunk

The potential harmful effects of alcohol use during pregnancy are well documented, and drinking alcohol during pregnancy is generally advised against. The risks of alcohol use while breastfeeding are less understood. Despite differences in opinion across the globe, the World Health Organization suggests avoiding alcohol completely during lactation. It can be a confusing call to make if you do want to enjoy an alcoholic drink occasionally. Speak to your midwife (or doctor), and assess how you feel once you've canvassed all the information you need.

Why did I [breastfeed] in public? Because I had to feed my child! It's unfortunate that people are so hard on women who choose to do it and do it in public.

MILA KUNIS

Baby-soft hands

You may find you're washing your hands more with the constant nappy changing. If as a result your hands are sore and dry, keep your favourite hand cream (preferably one scented with rose, jasmine or neroli for an immediate mood boost) by the sink, applying after every wash.

**Wouldn't it be cool if we treated
all postpartum moms and families
with awareness and honour?**

ALANIS MORISSETTE

Am I a good mum?

Are you a good mum? Yes, undoubtedly. Why? Because you care enough to ask the question. While it's not good to let self-doubt spiral, this sort of reflection only shows how much you love your child. And of course, you're not just a good mum because you worry about motherhood – you've got the actions to back it up, too! You're not skiving or doing the bare minimum like some indifferent, clock-watching office worker (chance would be a fine thing!). You're grafting day and night, quite literally, to meet the never-ending demands of your child. Your baby wants you above anyone else because you're meeting those needs, no matter what. On the days when you're disliking, resenting, even hating motherhood, this will always make you a good mum. Remember that.

WEEK FOUR

92

Age-old judgement

Around the world, pregnant women aged 35+ are considered "geriatric" (charming!) and, in some countries, more women are happily giving birth aged 35–39 than 20–24. So, why are "more mature mothers" still being made to feel like there's something wrong with them? A baby doesn't care about age. A baby needs love and nurture – let that (not outdated perception) be your guiding tenet in motherhood.

93

Young mum

Younger-than-average mums can experience stigmatizing attitudes just like older mums, when all that matters to a baby is having a nurturing presence. And how lucky is any child to be born into that sort of love?

My fingers are tickled to delight by
the soft ripple of a baby's laugh.

HELEN KELLER

Mum posture

It can be easy to fall into bad posture habits in the weeks after giving birth – when your body is inclined to slump naturally (it's even nicknamed "mum posture"!) due to physical and hormonal changes, typically resulting in a frontward pelvic tilt and rounded shoulders. Try to make a concerted effort to stand taller and keep your pelvis more aligned with your body, particularly when you're carrying your baby. Paying attention to your posture when you're prioritizing looking after a new baby can be tricky, but with practice it can become a habit you adopt without thinking.

Postnatal headaches

According to research, 39 per cent of new mums experience headaches often up to six weeks after giving birth, thanks to fluctuating hormones. Drinking lots of water, taking paracetamol and applying a drug-free headache balm can all be effective pain relief. For severe headaches, always speak to your midwife (or doctor).

Head in the clouds

A super-easy self-care technique is to stop what you're doing, even for a moment, and look up at the sky. Cloud watching is proven to have meditative effects on the body by immersing you in nature and momentarily putting your mind in a different headspace. For extra relaxation, try taking deep breaths as the clouds move across the sky, taking on different forms. It's a great way to de-stress on days fraught with tension.

Ear plug hack

A screaming baby can send stress levels soaring, particularly if incessant and for no apparent reason. It's perfectly natural to feel upset or anxious about this. Just remember it's very typical behaviour of a newborn to communicate anything and everything by means of wailing. Speak to your midwife (or doctor) if you're concerned. In the meantime, consider using earplugs to help reduce the noise and alleviate some of the stress. You're not ignoring your child! You're simply muffling the stress-inducing pitch, which can be a sanity-saver when you're trying to soothe a screaming baby.

I hope to teach my children that there is beauty in everything and everyone. I hope to teach them to focus on the beauty inside yourself and others, [rather] than what's on the outside.

MIRANDA KERR

Imperfection is perfection

"I just don't believe in perfection. But I do believe in saying, 'This is who I am and look at me not being perfect!' I'm proud of that." These words of wisdom uttered by Kate Winslet are spot-on. Striving for perfection, particularly as a new mum, is a roadblock for effective self-care. You need to cut yourself some slack and change your perception of imperfection. Review your day with a fresh perspective. House a mess? You have a home. Baby wearing a dirty onesie a little on the snug side? Your baby is clothed. Otherwise happy, healthy baby not established in any form of routine whatsoever? Your baby is thriving. And banish those books badgering you about routines! A perfect parent is a loving one simply doing their best.

Coconut delight

If you thought coconut oil was just for cooking, think again! It's also a brilliant makeup remover, lip balm, face mask and body and hair moisturizer. It even soothes dry scalp (a common mum-and-baby complaint) and treats nappy rash.

I went through a really hard time – I couldn't sleep, my heart was racing and I got really depressed. I went to the doctor and found out my hormones had been pummelled.

COURTNEY COX

Shades of postnatal depression

Gwyneth Paltrow has spoken openly about her experiences of PND, articulating brilliantly how symptoms often are not what you might expect: "I thought postpartum depression meant you were sobbing every single day and incapable of looking after a child. But there are different shades of it and depths of it, which is why I think it's so important for women to talk about it." How insightful! Never trivialize how you're feeling or think you're wasting anyone's time by opening up because, whatever the extent of your low mood, you don't have to cope alone.

In truth, I am a single mother. But I don't feel alone at all in parenting my daughter.

PADMA LAKSHMI

Co-parenting

If you're co-parenting your baby with a former partner, everything right now should revolve around your baby's feeding schedules (regardless of whether you're breast- or formula-feeding) and that vital bonding time between mum and baby. If an ex-partner isn't sharing a home with you and struggles seeing baby on an ad-hoc basis, effective communication will be key for you both to get through these early weeks. Be sympathetic and respectful, explaining that you understand how difficult it must be, but that ultimately baby's needs come first. Emphasize that this period is crucial but temporary and that you'd never want to deny your baby the chance of a good relationship with both parents. If talking directly to your ex-partner always dissolves into a row, communicate by text or email. Just keep the dialogue calm and considerate to set the precedent for a happy co-parenting relationship.

Carpal tunnel care

If you're experiencing any tingling, weakness, pain or numbness in your hands and fingers, then you may be suffering from carpal tunnel syndrome. The complaint is common during pregnancy, typically disappearing post birth, though it's not uncommon for a new mother to find that symptoms have stuck around or reoccurred – do seek advice from a doctor or physiotherapist if that's the case. In the meantime, try ice packs, elevating the affected arm as much as possible and using wrist splints to help alleviate symptoms.

All moms need confidants who can relate to what they're going through.

JESSICA ALBA

Treat your feet sweet

Plantar fasciitis is a common postnatal foot condition. The main symptom is stabbing pain in the heel or arch, often occurring in the morning. Fluctuating hormones are largely to blame, but increased body weight and swelling can also be contributory factors. Treat your feet to a pair of sturdy, supportive trainers to ease the pain; if that doesn't help and symptoms persist, your doctor may refer you to a physiotherapist or podiatrist.

Tray of treats

Around week four, many mums find that their babies start to feed for longer stretches, and what used to be roughly a half-hour session can last for two hours. While it's great that you and baby have established such an amazing feeding routine, when you're rooted to the spot for the duration, it can be quite debilitating (and yes, you're allowed to admit it, boring). Keep a tray of entertainment means (magazines, books, snacks, etc.) stationed at your go-to feeding spots around the house – all within reach and waiting for you for when those mammoth feeding sessions strike.

More sleep coming?

The great news for breastfeeding mums with babies now feeding for longer is that intervals between feeds will start to increase, and – wait for it – your baby is likely to sleep for longer, too. Your baby's tummy is still tiny, so it's unlikely they'll be able to sleep for more than a few consecutive hours at this age. Nevertheless, think of this as the holy grail of sleep looming on the horizon!

Partner talk

"I don't want to sleep like a baby. I want to sleep like my husband." This popular new-mum meme is like any good joke: it's funny because it's relatable. If, however, you're raising your baby with a partner who leaves most (or worse, all) baby-related matters to you, the joke starts to wear thin. The onus shouldn't be on you to "project manage" a partner to be more active in parenting. Even if you're breastfeeding or your partner has a full-time job, there are no excuses – a partner can still get up to burp or resettle a baby. Let's be frank: looking after the needs of a new baby *is* a 24/7 job.

Parenting is not babysitting!

"You're lucky your other half helps out with baby!" – No, you're not "lucky" to have a partner fulfilling parenting responsibilities. Parenting is not "helping out". When raising a baby with a partner, such attitudes are insulting to you both. Make this known to anyone who says otherwise.

With make-up

Wearing make-up can make you feel better as a new mum, as if you're reclaiming your pre-baby identity. The very process of applying make-up can also feel like an act of self-care, a soothing and relaxing means of self-touch. Whatever your reason for wearing make-up, negative comments by others are unacceptable. If you want to wear make-up, do it – and do it guilt free!

...Without make-up

Not every mum enjoys wearing make-up – whether that's down to a lack of time, energy or plain aversion to it. If you choose not to wear make-up, it's exactly that – *your* choice! A new mum's appearance is not open for discussion and there certainly shouldn't be any pressure to conform to any preconceived ideas of how a new mum should look.

**When you're up at three o'clock
in the morning, and they pee on
you, you just have to smile.**

WANDA SYKES

Feed when the baby feeds

It's not just "sleeping when baby sleeps" that's encouraged during these early weeks – it's eating, too. Firstly, the extra 500 or so calories burned through breastfeeding each day will likely leave you ravenous. Secondly, feeding yourself at the same time is a great way of freeing up precious time later on (and as a mum, you've no doubt already mastered the art of multitasking!). Obviously, trying to consume a scalding-hot meal with a baby on your breast is definitely not a good idea; instead, go for things like quartered sandwiches, frittata slices or small savoury tarts – great options for easy, baby-trapped meals.

Lactation cookies

Besides drinking the lactation smoothie, breastfeeding mums (and those pumping) might try boosting their milk supply by eating lactation cookies – no, not the average store-bought cookies loaded with sugar and high-fructose corn syrup, but the ones containing ingredients like flaxseed and brewer's yeast. Again, despite the name, they can be pretty delicious! Recipes proliferate online, but many shops sell them pre-made.

It occurred to me: I can stop breastfeeding.
That pressure is real, but what I realized
is that it was self-inflicted.

AMY SCHUMER

Express yourself

Exclusively pumping milk for your baby can leave you feeling exhausted and frustrated. Despite hours of expressing, you may find very little milk is produced, resulting in a "hangry" baby totally unfulfilled by the offering. The process alone (from pumping to sterilizing to storing) may prove overwhelming, but with the right equipment and a strong support network, things will improve. If you're exclusively pumping, it's worth asking your maternity team about borrowing a double pump, preferably a hospital grade one (they can be very expensive to buy otherwise). It may mean that you switch to formula. So what! A happy formula-feeding mum is worth so much more than a stressed breastfeeding mum!

Lactation consultant

Enlisting a lactation consultant (someone who specializes in supporting breastfeeding mothers) can bring comfort to new breastfeeding mums. Just check credentials, wherever you are in the world, to ensure you're getting the support you deserve.

Even in the most perfect circumstances, having a baby is a seismic shift in your life. Becoming a mother is the most profound thing I've experienced.

ELLIE TAYLOR

Bundle of joy

As any new mum will verify, it's hard not to chuckle when baby is attempting to gnaw its own foot for no apparent reason. It's also very hard to stifle a laugh when the concentration on baby's face suggests one thing: that poop is about to strike. And it takes enormous restraint not to hoot inappropriately when hungry baby roots at Granddad's chest for a feed. Such new parenting moments are comedy gold and ought to be preserved for life in your memory bank, ready to be withdrawn for an instant mood-lifter at any given moment. Seeing the funny in life is a proven effective self-care tool, improving our response to tension and even increasing our physical pain threshold.

ONE MONTH OLD

123

A month of being a mum!

Wow! You're the mother of a one-month-old baby! You've smashed the hardest newborn weeks. See that baby thriving? That's your hard work paying off right there.

124

Baby love

Sometimes, the most frustrating thing, when dealing with a newborn, is the lack of communication between you. Besides different crying cues, without actual words and obvious emotions for you to work with, your baby might well seem like a complete stranger. Except, your baby is communicating with you with every gaze. Even without that gummy smile (yet to turn your heart inside out), your baby is deeply in love with you.

Ditch the caffeine

Coffee and new motherhood are, for many mums, inseparable. But coffee can be entirely the wrong sort of fuel to reach for because caffeine blocks the effects of the sleep hormone adenosine – leaving you feeling alert after your morning cuppa, but more tired than before when it starts to wear off and the backlog of adenosine hits you all at once. Instead, fight the fug of fatigue with water, admittedly not as sexy as coffee, but when exhaustion is sapping you of energy (as it so often does when you're a new mum), something that's free and effective has to be a no-brainer.

I don't think we are responsible to anybody but our kids and ourselves.

BROOKE SHIELDS

Hormone fluctuations

Your emotions are still going through the wringer at this stage, thanks to fluctuating hormones and scant sleep. You might feel weepy, overwhelmed, irritable, anxious – a whole gamut of perfectly normal emotions – but just keep communicating how you're feeling because while it's all very common, it doesn't mean you should suffer alone.

128

Baby spam away!

Having witnessed a fair bit of spam in your time, you might have sworn in your childfree days that you'd never be the type to bang on about babies on social media. Perhaps now *you* are the baby spammer littering feeds with daily photo dumps from your phone? So what! For many mums, it's a means of connecting with people when leaving the house is tricky and rare. And being a proud new mother is never something to apologize for! So if posting pictures of your baby makes you happy, do it!

129

Stick your tongue out!

You may already be aware that when a newborn sticks their tongue out, it's often a sign they're hungry. But did you know that as they develop, it can also be a means of being playful? Try sticking your tongue out back and see if they copy; it's a cute form of early communication between you both and can provide sweet pockets of calm in the chaos.

I dig being a mother.

WHOOPI GOLDBERG

You will wake!

Studies have revealed that a baby's cry triggers stress hormones in mums, prompting them to soothe their infant. In fact, mums tend to respond within five seconds of hearing their baby cry, even if in a deep slumber. If worrying about not waking for your baby is robbing you of precious sleep, remember: no matter how deep the sleep you're in, you will wake for that baby; your instincts are strong.

Witching hour

Most new mums are familiar with Witching Hour, that excruciating time when babies around this age fuss for no obvious reason. The word "fuss" might even feel a little insufficient when a baby's scream feels fitting of a Hammer horror. Given that Witching Hour begins around 5 p.m., lasting until 11 p.m., the singular hour reference might also feel a bit like false advertising! Get as much help as you can to stay calm and hang in there – it'll pass in a few weeks and you'll be out the other side before you know it.

Motherhood is the most completely
humbling experience I've ever had.

DIANE KEATON

Write-ful thinking

Journaling has long been associated with catharsis and increased self-awareness. Albert Einstein, Nelson Mandela, Jennifer Aniston and Oprah Winfrey all have used it as a wellbeing tool. For many, it can provide a therapeutic source of managing stress, dumping worries and practising gratitude. Try adopting some writing prompts to help you focus on self-care on a regular basis. Perhaps start with a question like, "What positive parenting qualities make me unique?" Maybe list three things you're most proud of achieving today. Or complete the following sentence: "My baby is lucky to have me for a mum because..." Just don't put pressure on yourself to do it when exhaustion is sapping you of momentum. Only write when energy levels permit. And don't be modest! Positive self-talk is not about vanity – it's about emotional regulation and a productive frame of mind.

135

You're glowing

With your hormones all over the place and your body clearing excess fluid, you may be experiencing some night sweating. It's very normal, nothing to worry about, but can be a nuisance, especially when it's stopping you from sleeping. A fan for your bedroom (blowing on you, not baby) can bring sweet relief to night-time sweats. They should pass over the next couple of weeks, so don't (wait for it) sweat it!

136

Ah, babies! They're more than just adorable little creatures on whom you can blame your farts.

TINA FEY

137

Atrophy misery

Many new mums, breastfeeding ones in particular, can experience vaginal atrophy in the weeks after giving birth. If you're experiencing a very itchy or sore vagina, ask your midwife or doctor for help and make sure you get something specifically recommended or prescribed rather an impulsive over-the-counter or internet buy – you don't want to risk irritating the area further.

#Blessed

It's true: many of us are unlikely to chronicle on social media those moments when we're feeling like a hot mess, running late, dripping in sweat for baby clinic or resentfully wiping sick off your new top. But when you're scrolling through endless pictures of other mums seemingly breezing through new motherhood, it can be hard to see them (especially the commercially driven ones) for what they really are: a curated form of reality.

If your self-esteem slumps after spending time on social media, make a concerted effort to step away from your phone more. Better still, swerve depictions of new motherhood draped in designer labels and the kind of aesthetic a *Vogue* art director would envy, filling your feed instead with accounts that make you laugh and feel good. Your confidence is worth more than someone else's drive for social media engagement.

Sometimes the strength of motherhood
is greater than natural laws.

BARBARA KINGSOLVER

PJ days

Some days, especially during these early weeks, there's little to no chance of getting out of your pyjamas. Don't dwell on that. Try to embrace days like these for what they are: life with a newborn! Right now, when you're responsive to this little human's needs, some stuff just isn't a priority. This newborn period can be both frustrating and magical, but one thing's for sure: it's not forever.

Be kind to yourself

It might sound obvious, but adjusting to motherhood takes time. Think about it: one day you weren't a mother, the next (or maybe several, depending on your labour!) you were. And all the books, websites, magazines and advice in the world couldn't have prepared you for that. As many a mum will tell you, you have to live it in order to learn it. So, be kind to yourself. Every mother-and-baby journey is unique and yours is just beginning.

Nothing can really prepare you for it because you never again have a day where you don't think of your kids first.

ZOOEY DESCHANEL

TWO MONTHS OLD

Smile, baby!

Nope, it's not wind. It's not a reflex, either. It's baby's first genuine, unspeakably sweet social smile, making all those exceptionally challenging moments in motherhood *entirely* worthwhile. If you could bottle a baby's smile and sell it as self-care, you'd be a very wealthy person indeed!

Keep looking forward

If that first smile has got your heart soaring, wait until you hear that adorable laugh in about a month or two. Such new-parenting moments can wipe your memory clean of long days and sleepless nights, reminding you there's a lot of sunshine in store.

Baby must-have-nots

Wipe warmers, nappy bins, baby robes, dummy cases – the list of things you don't actually need for a baby is endless, not to mention expensive. Gadgets and products are likely to be marketed your way in the coming months as algorithms, as if by magic, pick up on the fact that you've got a new baby. But do you really need that baby blender for weaning when a cheap handheld one would suffice? What about that bottle warmer when a pan of water and a stove would work just as well? Pricey brand formula or the cheap stuff? Seriously! A baby is not going to sip the milk and ask what vintage it is...

Eight weeks in and I've taken a million vitamins, countless teas, lozenges, tinctures and worked with two lactation consultants. Breastfeeding. Is. Hard.

OLIVIA MUNN

Nap strike

There's nothing quite like an overtired baby refusing to nap to really push a new mum to her brink. There's a lot of eye rubbing going on, there's much yawning and the crying has reached a pitch that only dogs can hear, but still sleep doesn't come. And, wait for it – the baby's just as bad! When you've tried everything from swaying and singing to reading and rocking with no success, cut your losses and call off the battle with baby. The frustration in situations like these when your efforts seem futile can be pretty overwhelming, so get a change of scenery. Take a drive. Walk to the park. Maybe, with a bit of luck, your baby will fall asleep in the car or pram. The important thing is to keep moving and breathing deeply because there's not much to gain from staying at the scene of the crib-defying crime apart from soaring stress levels.

Why don't kids understand that their naps are not for them, but for us?

ALYSON HANNIGAN

Essential advice

There's a fair bit of evidence to suggest that by simply inhaling the aroma of rosemary essential oil, we can lower levels of stress hormone cortisol in our blood. When you feel stress escalating, apply a few drops to a clean flannel and inhale deeply before slowly exhaling. Do this four or five times in succession.

I read endlessly about pregnancy and what to eat and what not to eat [and] sort of prepared not at all for the actual baby.

ELLIE KEMPER

Desperately seeking serotonin

Mums who document a happy moment each day are thought to sleep better and feel more self-confident. Doing so may also boost levels of that all-important happiness hormone, serotonin. Try it! Every night, write a sentence about your day that makes you smile. It doesn't have to be about baby; managing to drink a whole cup of tea while still hot or visiting the lavatory unaccompanied by a clingy baby is a perfectly notable moment to celebrate in new motherhood!

Part-time clarity

If you're starting or returning to part-time work, make it very apparent (whether via email signature, out-of-office or by directly reminding your colleagues and employer) that you're uncontactable on your non-working days. It's really not OK for you to be working full-time when you're on a part-time salary.

Prep for running

If you're a fan of running and are keen to return to the pavements, it's generally recommended that mums wait at least 12 weeks post birth. Your bladder is likely to be quite leaky at this point, so it's a good idea to increase your Kegels ahead of running. Stock up on pads, too; you'll always be glad of the extra support!

Baby groups

Baby groups are not every new mother's cup of tea. And it's OK to admit to that. For some mums, they can feel overwhelming, cliquey and a little like being in a preschool TV show with nursery rhymes on loop and a lot of self-conscious dancing! If it's not your bag, why not make a call out on social media to see if any other mums you know fancy a coffee? If that doesn't suit, try a more structured, less pressured meetup like baby massage or a swimming class? These days, there are even apps for meeting other mums.

Kick off the conversation

Many mums feel shy about starting a conversation with another mother at a baby group. It's worth having a few stock questions at the ready – nothing intrusive or contentious obviously, just something like: "How old is your little one?" "Do you live locally?" "Have you been to many other baby groups?" Once you've broken the ice, conversation will follow and often, the other mother will be grateful for your effort.

(156)

You want to torture someone? Hand them an adorable baby they love who doesn't sleep.

SHONDA RHIMES

(157)

White noise

Some new mums swear by white noise machines as both a sleep aid and for calming fussing babies. With sounds replicating the noises a baby would have become accustomed to in the womb (including the mother's heartbeat), the idea is that a baby is comforted by the familiarity of it. Studies have shown that many colicky and acid reflux babies, in particular, appear to settle very quickly with the help of white noise and this can be a real sanity-saver for mothers struggling with nerve-shredding periods of the day and night. If you're keen to try a white noise machine, it's important to do your research and choose one that adheres to the recommended noise levels for a baby. It's also a good idea to attempt a few cheaper apps first to see what sounds are most effective for your baby; white noise, as a soothing means, won't work for all babies.

Loose skin

Loose skin around your belly after giving birth is very common (unsurprising, really, given you've literally just housed a baby!). The best course of action right now is patience. Whether you gave birth vaginally or via C-section, your skin's recovery is unique to you.

Stripes of pride

Truth be told, anything available over the counter is unlikely to help with the appearance of stretch marks. Those expensive creams promising to miraculously remove them aren't likely to do very much at all. The good news is that stretch marks will fade over the course of the year after giving birth. A dermatologist can perform treatments if they're bothering you, but try to change your perception; the medical term for stretch marks is "striae gravidarum" (Latin for "stripes of pregnancy"). They're simply your body's way of decorating you like a veteran of motherhood, and should be worn with pride.

I have to keep reminding myself that I created life, so if the repercussions of that are extra stretch marks [...] so be it.

ASHLEY GRAHAM

THREE MONTHS OLD

161

Back to work

According to one survey, two in five working mothers feel judged by their colleagues and seniors for finishing on time, demotivating them from seeking promotions. Working from home can make drawing that line between professional and family life even trickier. Establishing boundaries is essential for your mental health. From the outset, let people know when you'll be finishing. You can be polite and clear – just don't apologize. You're a mother who can't be all things to all people, and this is never something to be sorry for.

162

The moment a child is born, the mother is also born.

OSHO

Tomes of doom

Frantically flipping through pages of baby books searching for various explanations is a rite of passage for many new parents. If, however, these books are starting to feel like tomes of doom, with dogmatic age-specific milestones and stringent parenting rules, it might be time for less bossy bedtime books. Reading should be a joyous, non-judgemental experience!

Science of snuggles

There's nothing like a baby cuddle to take the edge off a bad day, is there? In fact, hugs are genuinely quite healing. According to scientists, they relieve stress, boost heart health, lower anxiety levels and produce oxytocin (the "cuddle hormone" causing a reduction in blood pressure and stress hormone norepinephrine). Oxytocin levels have been found to be particularly high when mothers hug their children. For optimum physical and mental wellbeing, pack in as many snuggles as possible with your gorgeous baby each day – as if you needed an excuse!

165

Bin the bulky bag

It's not uncommon for a new mum's pre-kids bag of choice (likely smart, fashionable and barely big enough for a hairbrush and cash card) to be booted for something about the size of a small car once baby comes along. Often, this is largely down to practicality, as nappies, cream, wipes, snacks, toys and countless other baby-related paraphernalia take precedence. However, lugging such bulky bags around won't be doing you any favours, particularly the mammoth, one-strapped monstrosities; you're better off using a backpack, which in spreading the weight evenly across your shoulders is much kinder to your back. Looking for an excuse to buy a new bag? Here it is!

166

Don't worry if your diaper bag isn't perfectly packed! As time went on, I started to just bring the essentials. I was like, "Let's just live life and not carry a million things around."

KOURTNEY KARDASHIAN

Breastfeeding is awesome. Formula is
awesome. Feeding your baby is awesome.
Not awesome? Judgement.

AMANDA SEYFRIED

Free to feed *anywhere*

If you're a breastfeeding mum and choose to nurse in public, NO
ONE should shame you or discourage you from doing so. Your
baby is hungry and in responding to your baby's needs, you're
keeping your baby alive. If someone has a problem, it's exactly
that: *their* problem. In many countries, anyone caught publicly
discriminating against a breastfeeding mum is breaking the law.

No formula shame!

Again, much like a breastfeeding mother, if you're a formula-
feeding mum, NO ONE has the right to subject you to stigma or
shame for how you feed your baby. When you're out and about
and formula-feeding your baby, just like the breastfeeding
mother, do so without apology. You don't owe anybody an
explanation; nourishing your baby is all that matters and it's no
one else's business how you go about doing that.

Maximize precious sleep

Research has shown that climbing into an unmade bed can increase stress levels, affecting quality of sleep. Talking about sleep quality might feel as worthwhile as discussing how best to serve a glass of water in a barren desert for some new mums, but it's worth heeding the benefits of making your bed first thing. Your sleep, no matter how scant, will stand to feel more restorative and you're more likely to kickstart your day with a productive, positive mindset.

Mother knows best

Nearly two thirds of new mothers feel they've been "mum-shamed" at some point during the first year of their baby's life, according to research. And the worst offenders? A new mum's own mother or a mother-in-law! It's likely not intended to be hurtful, but speak up and let your parent or in-law know how it's making you feel. Or ask a partner or relative to help. As mums themselves, your mother or mother-in-law should be able to relate and want to support you, so never presume it's not worth addressing.

Scalp massage

After everything it's been through, a new mum's body deserves some downtime. Show your body some appreciation for everything it's done for you with a gentle self-massage. Try this quick and simple exercise: apply light pressure with your fingertips to your scalp and, moving in a circular motion, inch slowly from your forehead to your neck. Do this for at least five minutes, taking care to cover your entire head. To increase the soothing sensation, try using almond or jojoba oil as you massage. It's also a great tip for thinning hair, common around three months after giving birth; one study found that after 24 weeks of daily scalp massaging, participants reported a boost in hair thickness.

Hair care

You can also take supplements to help with postnatal hair loss. If you're breastfeeding, look for new-mum specific treatments containing medically recommended levels of biotin.

**Your kid is only three months old.
Like, what are you going to the gym
for? Catch up on the [TV] reruns!**

ZOE SALDANA

Dress for *you*

When you're a time-poor new mum, it's not unusual to find your relationship with clothes changing. That basic button-up top may be a touch whiffy after four consecutive days of wear, but it's also very convenient for breastfeeding. Elasticated waistbands might have replaced your collection of beautiful belts, but comfort takes priority. Sure, that multi-pocketed hooded coat isn't your stylish denim jacket, but it feels like the safest bet as you leg it round town with a baby in tow.

Wardrobe shifts shouldn't be an issue, as long as you're being pressed towards more practical wear by necessity, rather than society. Dress for yourself, irrespective of what you think a "mum" should be wearing. Equally, if you're in the mood for hitting the supermarket in head-to-toe fashion fit for a catwalk, fill your trendy boots! Just live by *your* rules, not those dictated by some influencer or magazine.

It is a lovely thing to discover that your children don't want you perfect. They just want you honest. And doing your best.

ANGELINA JOLIE

Appy mother

There are now many apps designed to encourage self-care in new mothers; it's like having your own pocket cheerleader giving you mindful prompts, sleep deprivation advice, encouraging affirmations and stress-management suggestions. Some even offer a chance to meet a like-minded community of new mums through chat functions and networking, much like social media. Only opt for a reputable app that suits your emotional needs and personality, especially if it incurs a cost.

Tele-pram time

If your baby is prone to napping in the pram when you're out for a walk, why not use that time to call a friend or relative for a chat? These "tele-pram" moments can be useful for catching up and restoring connections you may be missing.

It is lonely at times and you do feel quite isolated, but actually, so many other mothers are going through exactly what you are going through.

CATHERINE, PRINCESS OF WALES

FOUR MONTHS OLD

(180)

Poonami warning

By now, you may have experienced your baby's "poonami" (an explosive bowel evacuation that fills the nappy). While completely normal, it's messy, never fun to deal with and likely to occur far from home. Packing spare nappies and clothes is about as much as you can do; this is a good metaphor for parenting life! Accepting the things beyond your control will help you to think rationally and, ultimately, move on.

(181)

Every day is something comical when you're raising kids. There's so much nonsense, whether it's what they're saying to you or the fact that there's avocado or poop on every surface.

KRISTEN BELL

Be honest

Ever noticed a social media post from a mum talking honestly about parenting getting a lot of engagement? Be it a celeb or an everyday post that's gone viral, mums tend to relate best to more authentic representations of motherhood. They're popular for a reason, often making the mums reading them feel less alone and more reassured that they're doing OK. Be a part of this new-mum revolution! We as humans are hardwired to protect our self-image, but talking truthfully about how we're feeling about motherhood (on or offline) will likely bring us closer to others feeling the same way, and that can only be a good thing.

Being a mom is incredibly challenging, but we still feel a pressure to talk about it in very romantic terms. We all have that resentment at times and anxiety about being trapped by the role.

CLAIRE DANES

Lemon lift

In need of a quick pick-me-up? Sniff a lemon! Studies have found the citrusy scent to boost energy and alertness, reduce stress and even improve self-image!

Phone away!

Smartphones can be hugely helpful in new motherhood, whether that's for online shopping, connecting with family and friends in seconds, instantly capturing milestone moments or even tracking your baby's development. However, much research suggests that excessive mobile phone use is linked to a range of mental health concerns, ranging from low self-esteem to loneliness to social phobia. Taking regular breaks from your phone can reduce the likelihood of your developing such conditions, while decreasing headaches, easing eye strain and simply helping you to inject some digital-real-life-balance into your life.

Sleep mode

Hanging up your handset is most crucial an hour before bed, scientists have found. The blue light emitted by your phone screen restricts the production of melatonin (the hormone responsible for the sleep cycle). This makes falling asleep trickier – not ideal when sleep is particularly precious. And, with that circadian rhythm disrupted, rising the following day can be tougher, too. Place it face down and out of reach to avoid absent-minded social media scrolling.

Wakey, wakey!

When you wake, whatever kind of night you've had, try to have a good old stretch before even poking a toe outside the duvet! Stretching first thing can help to relieve any tension after a slumber. When you sleep, your muscles lose tone and fluid tends to pool along your back. Stretching helps to gently massage that fluid back into its normal position. As many new mums will attest, a night of disrupted sleep can result in an extra cranky body and mood to match – so get stretchy, not tetchy!

Morning routine

Establishing a routine typically goes out the window when you're a new mum. But, even a small morning routine can create a sense of calm. Drink a glass of water first thing (sleep deprivation has been linked to dehydration); step into your garden or stick your head out the window, breathing in some morning air; then hit the kitchen for a brain-boosting glass of carrot and orange juice, followed by a good breakfast (see tip 193) to kickstart your day.

Drive-by mum shaming

As many a mum will you tell, unsolicited advice is not the only judgement a new mother can be subjected to; often there's a more passive-aggressive, almost blink-and-you'll-miss-it drive-by form of shame to contend with, too. Comments like, "Personally, I'm very against dummies, but if you're comfortable with them, that's great!" and "Gosh, you've got make-up on – how wonderful to have some time on your hands!" are, by their gaslighting, drive-by nature, hard to confront. If ever you're on the receiving end of them, the only shame you should be feeling is for them.

Shaming other mothers is not one of the million ways to be a great mom.

BRENÉ BROWN

Candy girl

Multiple studies have shown that many new mums have a much sweeter tooth after giving birth, due to a vitamin or mineral deficiency (typically magnesium). It's always worth investigating with a health professional if you're deficient, but in the meantime, try satisfying those hankerings with a sticky Medjool date or two squares of good quality dark chocolate (without the nasty blood sugar spike).

It's the most empowering feeling, because it makes you want to worry about the pettiness and trivial things a lot less.

KELLY CLARKSON ON MOTHERHOOD

Breakfast boost

A round of white toast dripping with butter or a bowl of sugary cereal might be tempting and convenient when you're short of sleep and energy, but both are unlikely to be doing you any favours in the self-care stakes. While it's hard to stifle a yawn at the typical high-fibre and low-sugar alternatives in tedious brown packaging on the supermarket shelves, these really are the better options. If the thought of kickstarting your day with something boringly virtuous makes you balk, then get creative. Smashed avocado on a piece of granary toast, for instance, is an easy meal packed with vitamin C, potassium, fibre and flavour. If this feels like too much of a faff on particularly sluggish mornings, swap the avocado for nut butter and top with your favourite fruit. A quick search online will reveal hundreds of energy-boosting breakfast ideas for after broken, baby-busy nights.

Back off, grandma!

Rudely asking an overbearing grandparent to stop undermining or interfering with your parenting is unlikely to go down well. Instead, aim for a peaceful resolution. The likelihood is that their intention, however forceful, is well-meant. Make the boundaries clear by reiterating politely that you're the mother. Thank them for their help or advice and say politely: "My baby is so lucky to have such a giving grandparent. I'm going to take on board what you've said and all you've done and take it from here." Charm, disarm, keep calm!

Own the room

A grandparent uncomfortable at the sight of a new mum breastfeeding can be a tricky problem to navigate, especially when generational and cultural beliefs are ingrained into that unease. It's still your call to make, no one else's. Rather than indulge this sort of behaviour, just let *them* leave the room; your hungry baby takes priority.

We all have nipples. I don't care who
I offend; my baby wants to eat.

SELMA BLAIR

Sisterhood solidarity!

Have you ever noticed that famous childfree men are rarely asked to elaborate on their plans for procreation? Celebrity childfree women, on the other hand, are frequently scrutinized for leading lives without kids: "Has she chosen a career over babies?" "Can she have children?" "Doesn't she like kids?" If you or perhaps someone you know has ever experienced anything similar, you'll know how exhausting and intrusive it can be. It's no one else's concern why a woman does not have kids and if a relative or friend in your circle is being subjected to such scrutiny, whether directly or indirectly, try to speak up for her. It feels good to be sympathetic like this. And of course, deterring unnecessary speculation about a woman's fertility and procreation plans benefits all women.

My choice to be childfree gets questioned by strangers like they're the CIA and I'm a suspect who isn't giving them the whole story.

JEN KIRKMAN

Healing hands

When you're feeling emotional, don't underestimate the power of touch. We all hold our stress and nervous tension in different parts of the body: for many of us, it's the neck and shoulders, for some, the lower back, for others, the scalp. If finding time seems impossible, even asking a partner, relative or friend to give you a back rub can make such a difference when your body's feeling tense.

It's only now that I no longer count other people's children or judge myself harshly for not providing my daughter with a sibling.

EMMA THOMPSON

Having another?

Before a new mum's stitches have even had a chance to heal, questions about plans for a second baby may need fielding. Such interrogation is totally inappropriate! If it makes you uncomfortable, don't be afraid to make your feelings known: perhaps change the subject, find an excuse to leave the room, say you feel a bit awkward about the question... Just remember you're under no obligation to answer such impertinent questions.

FIVE MONTHS OLD

(202)

Weaning your way

Thinking about weaning methods? Remember: it's *your* decision to make. Whether you're veering more to baby-led weaning or spoon-feeding, bossy, unsought advice can test a new mum's patience. So, be firm, explaining you're only interested in qualified sources. If you prefer, simply smile and subtly change the subject. Just nip that overbearance in the bud early, reminding yourself that you and you alone will choose what's best for your baby.

(203)

Food for thought

Choose weaning recipes that make *your* mouth water, too! Introducing solids to your baby's diet is priority, but there are many foods, even at the preliminary stage of weaning, that a new mum can tuck into alongside baby.

Stop telling mums what to do with their kids! All kids are different.

CARDI B

Library love

If you're lucky enough to have a local library, join it! Libraries can be a fantastic sanctuary for a new mum in search of friendship and activity outside the house, with many offering baby groups and children's story times. Plus, it's a wonderful source of FREE books for both you and baby!

Music is key

Experts have found that music can lift a listless mood in seconds. Just those first few bars of your favourite track, particularly if it's an up-tempo one, can drive out despondency and motivate you into action in much the same way as it incites a faster pace in the gym. And, according to numerous studies, a sing-a-long could enhance your mood further by boosting immunity, mental alertness, lung function and those ever-essential endorphins. So what if your singing voice is like a howling hyena; as long as your effusive efforts aren't in danger of waking a sleeping baby, then who cares!

Sun block

Blackout blinds tend to feature high on the nursery shopping list. Yet, research has shown that we all could benefit from sleeping in a darkened environment. For a cheaper alternative, a simple eye mask can work just as effectively.

Quick meditation

Quick fix meditation is great for bringing moments of calm into your everyday self-care routine, but for the biggest rewards, it's still worth dedicating a decent amount of time to mastering it. The good news is that meditation is not as rule-bound as you might think. Try this mindful meditation routine (which can be practised anywhere): choose a natural object from your immediate environment and focus on it; look at this object as if you're seeing it for the first time, visually exploring every aspect of it for as long as your concentration can manage; finish by closing your eyes, inhaling deeply to the count of five and exhaling slowly as you open your eyes.

Motherhood unlocked new levels of
respect I have for my mommy!

RIHANNA

Mindful walking

The future can feel fraught with frightening possibilities when the responsibility of a baby weighs heavy. If you're in need of allaying an anxious mind, try living in the moment. The next time you go for a stroll with baby, pay closer attention to your surroundings, absorbing as much detail as possible (from big buildings to beautiful birds). Breathe slowly and deeply, absorbing the sounds as you observe. The more you practise mindful walking, the easier it'll be to mute those unfounded future fears.

Booked up

If, as a result of sleep deprivation and having barely enough time to read a cereal packet, your relationship with reading has waned, now might be the time to dip back in. Incorporating into your daily routine as little as six minutes of reading can improve quality of sleep, reduce stress (audiobooks, in particular, can help to reduce negative thinking), sharpen mental acuity and lower heart rate and blood pressure. Crucially, reading is pleasurable and in new mum self-care terms, something enjoyable for yourself.

Solo warriors

Raising children (particularly a new baby) alone means you need more than sympathetic smiles and well-intended remarks – you need a helping hand. Assuming the role of breadwinner *and* homemaker makes tending to your self-care needs even harder. And all the more necessary. If you're parenting without a regular support network, try building one. Suggest regular playdates with another parent. Ask a relative or friend to sit with your baby while you nap. Source single-parent sites and apps for advice and camaraderie. Never be afraid to ask for help because even warriors get tired.

I am prouder of my years as a single mother than of any other part of my life.

J. K. ROWLING

Memo to self

As any child of a single parent will tell you, the bond is like no other. "Sometimes, I cannot put into the words how much I love her," said British footballer Marcus Rashford of his mum (who raised him and his siblings alone). What you and your baby are forging together is second to none. Never forget this.

Money matters

Raising a family isn't cheap, is it? Excluding typical costs (bills, food, mortgage/rent, etc.), the average parent spends around half their annual income on their children's needs. It can be hard to stay on top of finances when raising your costly baby is pretty time-consuming. Thankfully, many interactive tools can help you to manage money matters, from banking apps tracking your account daily to budget organizers ensuring you spend within your means. A search online could also reveal the benefits you're entitled to, so it's worth exploring all your options. If financial difficulty is causing you concern, do reach out for support. There are many cost-free organizations that can help, so don't think you have to go through it alone.

Clothes swap

If frequently forking out for baby clothes is clocking up a monumental amount of money, why not host a clothes swap party and invite friends with babies of varying ages? It's not just great for cost cutting, but also a means of decluttering outgrown clothes and meeting other new mums.

Tub therapy

As a new mum, taking a bath can feel very indulgent. But it's not as if you're Cleopatra bathing in ass's milk. It's self-care with scientifically-proven benefits. In fact, a long soak in the tub can improve your blood flow and (when you're breathing deeply and slowly) oxygenate your blood. It can also lift low mood, build immunity by killing bacteria, alleviate muscle pain and improve sleep. So ditch the guilt and dig out the rubber duckie.

Foot bath

If a soak in the tub isn't a likely option, immersing your feet in a bowl of warm water can induce similar effects: reducing inflammation and stimulating circulation. Reflexologists also suggest adding a few drops of lavender oil for extra therapeutic benefits.

My family is blended and diverse and nutty, and loving and understanding. That's a family.

SANDRA BULLOCK

**Being a mother is the best opportunity and
challenge I've ever been blessed with in life.**

JESSICA SIMPSON

Breast engorgement

If you're a breastfeeding mum and your baby is now sleeping
for longer, you might be experiencing some breast engorgement
(when your breasts become overfull with milk). If as a result
you're feeling any discomfort, pump regularly to ease the swelling
and invest in some ice packs. Painkillers can also help. If you're
concerned, speak to a healthcare professional, but rest assured,
this will pass and your body will adapt to your baby's needs.

Mummy's milestones

Forget baby milestones, what about your milestones? Managed
to leave the house before midday? Stop by your favourite shop.
Prepared and finished a sandwich while seated (instead of
dining on ham straight from the packet by an open fridge door)?
Treat yourself to a chocolatey dessert. Seriously, stop and look at
how far you've come. Moments like these might have felt totally
unattainable just a few short months ago, but those gear changes,
however seemingly trivial, are happening because of you. You're
rocking this parenting lark – make sure you acknowledge and
celebrate that.

SIX MONTHS OLD

(223)

Happy half year!

Congratulations! You've been a mother for half a year. Toast this six-month milestone. You deserve it – and you need to tell yourself that.

(224)

Friend request

Studies have shown that in order to thrive socially, relationships need to be based on more than simple companionship. Your endorphin levels and mental wellbeing, even your immune system, benefit from the presence of strong, likeminded alliances. It's OK to be discerning about friendship beyond having babies born around the same time. Let's be honest, a decent belly laugh relieves a stressful day far more than a dry conversation about milestones ever could.

Good company

"I have insecurities of course, but I don't hang out with anyone who points them out to me." Singer Adele couldn't have put the art of choosing the company we keep better. As a new mum, it's important to surround yourself with the right people for you. The saying, "You can't pick your family, but you can choose your friends" is very true. Vow to spend time with the people who big you up, not put you down.

Office junior

If you're on maternity leave and planning to pop into your place of work to introduce your baby to your colleagues, it might be a good idea to talk it through with a trusted co-worker first. Get a sense of when would be best, and if you're feeling nervous at all about it, ask if they could meet you beforehand. Remember, you're under no obligation to do the baby meet-and-greet, so if you'd rather not, don't!

One way of life

Tiger mum. Helicopter mum. Attachment mum. Mum stereotypes like these are just that: stereotypes. Ignore the labels because there's only one way to parent – *your* way!

The majority of my diet is made up of the foods that my kid didn't finish.

CARRIE UNDERWOOD

My space

Look around your home. Perhaps the interior you so carefully fashioned from every imaginable swatch and pages of a Swedish furniture catalogue is now drowning in a sea of baby paraphernalia? That may be the standard in the early days of motherhood, but it doesn't mean you can't salvage a space of sanctuary for yourself. Carve out an area, a room if you can, and fill it with some of your favourite things (comfy cushions, scented candles, a good book, perhaps) – anything that creates calm and serves as a reminder of your sense of identity. Use this space as often as tending to a tiny human permits and each time, consider it a small moment of baby-free restoration.

Weaning support

Weaning proving troublesome? Canvas tips from your midwife or doctor. You will get through this and your baby will be chowing down like a champ before you know it – just don't be afraid to lean on the people there to help.

Forum caution

The internet can be a new mother's best friend *and* worst enemy (particularly when it comes to online mum forums). Treat advice offered on mum forums carefully. And remember, it's you (not some stranger in a forum) who decides how best to raise your baby.

Unless you are [my child's] doctor, father, or mom, do NOT tell me how to raise my child, or how to feed her.

JANA KRAMER

Pick up the pace

When exhaustion is shredding your last nerve, putting on a pair of trainers and pounding round the park might seem about as appealing as a visit to the dentist. This could be exactly what you need, though. Cardiovascular exercise has been proven to increase energy levels by boosting your body's oxygen circulation. This surge in oxygen allows your body to function better and, in turn, use its energy more efficiently. Benefits also include an increase in endorphins, a sharper focus and improved sleep. If your fatigue is all-consuming or time is particularly tight, a brief walk can still generate plenty of health gains. Psychologists report that just ten minutes of walking at a brisk pace can provide the same stress relief as a 45-minute workout. So the next time you're heading out for a coffee morning or nipping out for a loaf – pick up the pace! It all counts.

Running is the basis of all the training
that I do... It's like an escape.

ELLIE GOULDING

Shower meditation

Contrary to stereotype, meditation doesn't have to be practised in an incense-filled room. It can actually be incorporated into a new mum's chaotic life – even in the shower. The next time you take a shower, face the water and close your eyes. Take a few deep breaths, focusing on the feeling of expansion as you inhale and the sense of tension relief, as you exhale. Slowly turn away from the water and repeat, noting how the water feels on your back as your breathe. Continue this for a couple more minutes. Sure, it's no Thailand retreat, but it is an easy and effective self-care exercise that'll bring you some soothing meditative benefits in minutes.

A gripping tale

If you have long hair and it's become a source of fun for your baby's developing grip, get in the habit of tying it back. Postnatal hormones are still making your luscious locks a little fragile – plus it *really* hurts!

**Having children made me realize
how making the world a better
place starts at home.**

MADONNA

Show yourself some love

Ever noticed how cosy it is to roll out of bed on a cold, frosty morning and slip into a pair of warm slippers? Positioning those slippers at your bedside the night before is like a little act of self-kindness. So too is leaving your favourite mug sitting by the kettle – teabag and spoon all set for a comforting cuppa. Dotting signals around the house that nudge you into self-care mode will remind you that you matter as much as your baby. Vow to do one thing, entirely for yourself, each day.

I love being a mom! It's the most rewarding feeling! You have to remember though, to make time for yourself.

KIM KARDASHIAN

Break for tea

A university study has found that tea drinkers are calmer and less prone to depression than coffee drinkers; the reason being that amino acid theanine in tea has stress-reducing qualities. You're also less likely to suffer from restlessness, headaches and sleep disruption with tea, due to its lower caffeine content.

Everything's a phase!

It's highly unlikely your baby will start secondary school with a soother. It's probably safe to say your child won't need to be swayed to sleep at the age of 30. Chances are, you won't need to go to your child's place of work every lunchtime to feed them purée, airplane style. Babies develop at their own pace; whenever a stage or phase is preying on your mind, remind yourself of this.

Embrace your mood!

From broken sleep to teething to weaning, a new mother can face a number of challenges along with a gamut of negative emotions. Rather than suppress your feelings, embrace that bad mood because you're a human being and like your baby, your emotions need expressing! Let people know when you're feeling fed up. Talk it out with a friend or relative. People, particularly other new mothers, will get it and might even want to offload, too. Most importantly, remember that repression is a barrier to robust mental health, and moving away from it is essential for effective self-care.

SEVEN MONTHS OLD

243

Postpartum is very real. And there's
so many resources that we just have
to help each other find what they are
and keep getting the word out there.

REESE WITHERSPOON

244

Postnatal depression

It's a common misconception that PND only occurs soon after
giving birth, when in fact one in six mothers experiences the
condition months after childbirth. If you're frequently suffering
from mood swings, crying spells, anxiety and difficulty sleeping,
talk to your maternity team about how you're feeling. With
prompt treatment, you will get through this. Just remember: in
order to care for your baby, you need to take care of yourself first.

I too struggled with depression after my first baby was born. To those of you going through this, know that you're not alone and that it really does get better.

SARAH MICHELLE GELLAR

Morning walk

Lots of new mums with sleep-reluctant babies will be familiar with rude dawn awakenings. The temptation might be to shuffle to the kitchen for extra-strength coffee to slurp in front of breakfast TV, when actually you'd benefit more from a walk within the first hour of waking. Morning light has been proven to clear sleep hormone melatonin out of the bloodstream, giving your brain the clarity it needs to focus. Your vitamin D, serotonin and blood pressure levels will stand to benefit, too.

Mid-morning munchies

When a mid-morning slump has you rummaging in the cupboards for sustenance, pass up the carby treats for a protein-based snack, by far the better choice in the energy stakes. A big handful of nuts or some peanut butter on celery is bound to slay a slump.

Hydro power

Water is a hugely underestimated fatigue fighter, with many experts recommending a glass of water every hour for a noticeable boost in energy levels. Try getting into the habit of stationing glasses of water about the house, particularly where you're likely to be feeding your baby; you should begin to feel a difference within just a few days.

Channel the positive

Television may be touted as a source of "brain rot", but recent research suggests watching feel-good shows can actually have a relaxing effect on the body and boost positive emotions. According to psychologists, "nostalgia television" (your favourite shows from childhood) can be a great source of therapeutic comfort. So, if a little boxset binge on the sofa post bath and bedtime has become your downtime routine, don't consider this a mindless activity. As long as you're not watching too much TV late at night (linked to sleep disturbance, anxiety and low mood), you can disregard the stigma and slump in front of the small screen to de-stress!

The not-to-do list

Folding the laundry can wait! Don't bother drying the dishes! Underpants don't need to be ironed! Scratch all unnecessary household chores off your list because that time could be freed up for an episode of your favourite TV show or precious chapters in a brilliant book.

I want my girls to see the model of a mother taking care of herself, because, quite frankly, my mother didn't do that.

MICHELLE OBAMA

Vitamin vitality

When you're a new mum, it's easy to neglect your nutritional needs, but be sure to nourish your body the same way you would your baby's; supplementary vitamins can offer a real boost. It's important to evaluate how you feel to determine the best route. Do also check in with your doctor, especially if you're overwhelmingly sluggish, anaemic or suffering from frequent headaches.

Mother superior

Maybe there's another new mum you know who seems to be coping very well with motherhood? Perhaps you've enviously observed an energetic demeanour and listened to tales of restful nights and struggle-free routines? In reality, that mum is probably contending with similar insecurities just like you. Try to resist comparing yourself unfavourably to other mothers – especially when those feelings of inadequacy are completely unfounded.

You can't "spoil" babies!

Fact: you cannot hold or hug a baby too much. Scientific research has shown that babies thrive on closeness to their mothers. If it's ever suggested that you're somehow "spoiling" your baby with too many hugs, explain that there is zero, nada, NO way you can spoil a baby with love.

I think bringing a life into this world is the single most important thing a person can undertake, and it can also be the most challenging. I think as mothers we are all just trying our best.

GISELE BÜNDCHEN

Recreating romance

When you're raising a baby with a partner, it can become very easy to slip out of the habit of making time for each other. If romance has been replaced by perfunctory conversations about nappies, it might be time to review the situation. OK, tending to a new baby leaves little room for nipping to Paris to sip champagne, but when the chaos relents (which it will), simply booking a babysitter and hitting the local can be a real tonic for you both. Even recreating a date night at home with a film and posh supper can be all it takes to remind yourselves, lovely as it is, that there's more to your relationship than being parents.

[My husband] and I still try to have date nights. When you've had a week of little sleep, you can get into a rut, so having one night where you can chat again means you're a bit fresher.

ALEX JONES

Baby books of lies!

"By seven months, babies typically sleep about 11 hours at night – many straight through – and take two daily naps that add up to three to four hours." Perhaps this is the kind of thing your baby book says? Bin that big book of baby lies! A baby's development is unique and (especially when it comes to sleep routines) rarely "typical". If your baby is nowhere near sleeping like this, don't sweat it! Hopefully more respite (even if not remotely resembling what a book or website says) is a sign of things to come!

Breaking yawn

Some researchers believe that yawning leads to an increase in heart rate and the release of wake-promoting hormones. Looking for a quick hit of energy? Yawn away! Although, let's be honest, as the mother of a young baby, it's probably stifling a yawn that's harder to do...

People who say they sleep like a
baby usually don't have one.

LEO J. BURKE

261

Plant power

Being surrounded by indoor plants works wonders for your wellbeing, increasing your attention span by around 20 per cent and improving mood and memory. So, dot a few around your home. Quick tip, though: go for low-maintenance plants like cacti and dragon trees; you want plants to enhance your energy levels, not drain them (the last thing you need as a new mum!).

262

There's no right and wrong. There's just different children.

NICOLE KIDMAN

263

#Parentingfail

The online mum world has its issues, but against the #gifted posts, smug selfies and parenting police is the antithesis of perfect parenting: mums sharing social media posts of their bad days (including their failures). This sort of camaraderie can work wonders for a new mum's self-esteem. Wishing you were anywhere but home during Witching Hour? You're not alone. A coffee-shop meet-up cut short by a sudden poonami and no spare clothes? Laugh! Because "parenting fails" aren't fails at all – they're just part of the everyday life of the average, honest mum.

Teatime for me time

Research shows that tea drinking rituals are as important for reducing stress as the tea itself. Ritualizing your tea break is mindfully committing to that respite in your day when you can enter a more relaxed, reflective headspace. Perhaps a good time to do this is when baby is napping or sitting happily in a bouncer. Slow the tea-making process down (perhaps using a teapot and a cup and saucer), listen to your favourite playlist and light a candle. Just design your ritual to feel like a pause in your day when you focus solely on yourself.

Tooth hurty

Teething ring! Check. Baby paracetamol? Check. Dental gel? Check. Now, where's your pain relief? It's heart-wrenching to see your little cherub gnawing at their favourite toy, desperately trying to relieve the miserable pain that comes with teething, but it can take its toll on you, too. If it feels like you've regressed to those newborn days of sleepless nights and endless crying, call in the cavalry and don't forget *you*.

Mind your own!

However you conceived (be it through IVF, with a partner, whatever) and whether or not you gave birth with an epidural, remember: it's *your* business. If you find someone's line of questioning impertinent, master, in whichever way you're most comfortable, ways of shutting that conversation down. You're under no obligation to oblige someone else's intrusiveness.

Biology is the least of what makes someone a mother.

OPRAH WINFREY

Their own person

"Doesn't she look like her uncle?" "He's the spit of his dad!" "It's like looking at Great Aunt Miriam!" People can't help but draw physical comparisons between a baby and other family members. However well-intended, such comparisons can drive a new mum to distraction. If you're regularly gritting your teeth over this, just say: "My baby looks like my baby." After all, everyone, identical twins included, is unique and babies don't need to be physically aligned to an existing or late family member to be understood.

Little souls find their way to you whether they're from your womb or someone else's.

SHERYL CROW

Soothing scent

If you thought burning candles for relaxation was a load of new-age nonsense, think again. The flickering flame of a candle is scientifically proven to reduce stress; it may even help you to reach a more meditative state. That's because our brains associate the low light with relaxation, making us feel more tranquil. Our immune system and mood improve as a result, and we sleep better, too. Some studies have shown that candles with a soothing scent like lavender or chamomile can drive down further those stress levels brought about by cortisol. After baby's bath and bedtime, light a candle and mindfully observe it, inhaling the scent. Take note of how you feel afterwards. It might be that you need to try a few different fragrances until you find your fit, but keep with it – the stress-relieving benefits may surprise you.

Positive perspective

When you're in the middle of a difficult phase, it's easy to become so fixated on your current situation that you lose sight of the positives. Neuroscientists have discovered that by simply allowing your brain to think positively, things feel less overwhelming. That's because thinking positively sends a surge of calming neurotransmitter enkephalin into your brain. Try flipping negative thoughts into positive ones, perhaps when baby's going through a stage of being super clingy. Rather than feel annoyed, simply change the way you look at it, seeing it instead as precious cuddle time you'll never get back again.

Who loves ya, baby?

"To the world, you are a mother, but to me, you are the world." This anonymous quote epitomizes that moment when a baby's face lights up and breaks into a gorgeously gummy smile at the sight of mum. This is the unconditional love you give reflected right back at you, and these are the moments to preserve in your memory bank – moments that can turn even the most testing of days around.

EIGHT MONTHS OLD

273

Mum on the town

If you're planning your first night out as a mum, it's perfectly natural to feel a little anxious about it. OK, you might text your partner or babysitter 27 times to check in. Yes, you may blub because your emotions are more erratic than a toddler presented with the wrong colour beaker. There's absolutely nothing wrong with any of this! Just consider it a rite of new-mum passage and trust that you'll eventually relax.

274

Regular night out

Studies suggest socializing with friends twice a week to feel the chemical benefits of human interaction. That frequency is pretty unlikely with a new baby! However, with whatever sort of regularity you can manage, just make it fun and friend-filled.

Baby talk

When you're the mother of a young baby, conversations about "who's got your nose" can be somewhat limiting. Sweet as they are, such chats don't quite cut the mustard when you're in the mood for a bit of political discourse or a conversation about last night's TV. Experts suggest avoiding the dreaded new-mum burnout by engaging in adult conversation on a regular basis. Discussions about noses and blowing raspberries will be much easier to cherish when it's not the defining conversation of your day!

Only I can understand my kid. She's like, "BDIDKDKODKDHJXUDHEJSLOSJDHDUSJ MSOZUZUSJSIXOJ" and I'm like, "OK I will get you a piece of sausage in just a minute."

CHRISSY TEIGEN

Puzzling matters

Like many new mums, you may be experiencing "brain fog" more than before. But puzzling can help! Participants of one study who regularly engaged with puzzles exhibited the brain function of someone ten years younger. If uttering "what was I saying?" is taking over your life, remember: a puzzle a day helps keep the brain fog away!

Forest bathing

According to Japanese scientific studies, being amid trees can help reduce stress, blood-pressure levels and heart rates. While out walking with your baby, wander through a tree-filled park or local woods if you can, pausing regularly for deep breaths. Apparently, frequent "forest bathers" report feeling a greater sense of wellbeing and optimism – so get tree hugging!

Switch off

Living on a commune with a herd of unicorns might seem more feasible right now than finding time for solitude. But even 15 minutes can be enough to disarm tension. The key is to switch off (your phone, the TV, radio, laptop – unplug them all). Sit somewhere comfortable, close your eyes and consciously navigate your thoughts (plan these thoughts ahead if it helps) towards a happy place. Try to do this regularly and, if at all possible, at the same time, thinking of it as a power-saving state to conserve energy.

Blooming lovely

Ever "stop and smell the roses"? This phrase is worth taking literally. Experts have found that the perfume of certain flowers (including roses) can give your brain a boost. Roses give off a fragrance that, for many, spells summer (longer, warmer, brighter days). So too does jasmine, also said to help with sleep, and lisianthus, believed to aid creativity. The scent of chrysanthemums has even been known to lower stress levels. So show yourself some love with a beautiful bunch of blooms once in a while.

Not *just* a mum

How many times have you heard a mother describe themselves as "just a mum"? It's a common habit of mums without a job outside motherhood. However, as you've probably learned already, being a mum is by no means easy, but one of the hardest jobs in the world. Whenever you refer to yourself as a mother, say it with complete pride – always omitting "just".

"Oh, I'm just a mom," you hear women say. *Just* a mom? Please! Being a mom is everything. It's mentorship.

SALLY FIELD

Boogie, baby!

No matter your ability or talent, there's nothing like a dance to see off a bit of despondency. None of this shoulder-shimmying nonsense, either – really get your groove on! Vigorously moving as much as physically possible can improve your heart health, muscle strength, balance and coordination. It's even been scientifically proven to reduce depression. So, when a funk strikes, bop to a kitchen or lounge disco, with or without a baby on your hip, and feel those endorphins hike in just 30 minutes.

A mother's love liberates.

MAYA ANGELOU

Bed before midnight

Sleep experts have discovered that our bodies respond to changing light levels in the evening, when your body is preparing for some shutdown. This makes the hours before midnight the most powerful phase for sleep. Even if your relationship with sleep is a little iffy thanks to a kip-reluctant baby, you can deposit twice the amount in the snooze bank if you nod off before 12. That has to be worth an early night!

Supermarket sanctuary

Remember when a supermarket grocery shop was a chore – something you were keen to get over and done with as quickly as possible? Chances are, you're now nostalgic for those carefree days when you could shop in peace without fear of a bawling baby or sudden need to source baby-changing facilities. A trip to the supermarket *without* baby, as many mums will attest, practically feels like a spa break! Where possible, seize any opportunity to go wild in the aisles alone, whether that's perusing new foods or leisurely treating yourself to a magazine or newspaper. The supermarket, once a source of stress, is now a potential place of sanctuary...

Shopping hack

If food shopping with baby is unavoidable and you fear a meltdown might strike, try planning ahead as much as possible to keep your shopping trip brief. A handy hack is to write your list in order of the supermarket aisles so you can zip through the items you need at lightning speed.

Motherhood has a very humanizing effect. Everything gets reduced to essentials.

MERYL STREEP

Off sick

"Oh, hello, baby. Mummy, here. Unfortunately, I'm feeling unwell today, so I won't be able to look after you. I've put my out-of-office on and will catch up with everything on my return. I'll let you know when I'm feeling better, OK? Bye now!" Calling in sick when you're a new mum is not really happening, is it? Babies aren't exactly deterred by your exhausted, red-nosed face when the need for a feed or potent nappy change strikes. However, it's important to accept that you can't carry on regardless. Enlist some extra childcare support if possible, or let a few things slide. Again, the dirty dishes can wait. An online supermarket delivery can plug any grocery gaps. Canned soup will suffice for dinner. Just focus on getting as much rest as possible when you're feeling unwell.

You look great!

If you're looking through photos of yourself with baby and responding with a self-deprecating remark about your image, vow to stop that now. You've carried and birthed life – you are AMAZING. Refrain from magnifying what *you* consider to be body negatives because those early photos of mother and baby are so beautiful and momentous, they should be treasured as such.

Take the compliment!

Hearing you're doing a great job can mean a lot to an insecure new mum. If someone remarks on how well you're doing, heed this. Research has shown that women are more prone to rejecting compliments, which is bad practice for boosting self-esteem. Say thank you and deposit that compliment in your bank of self-worth.

As a new mom, it was important to hear compliments from people, like, "Hey, you're doing a great job." Those went such a long way, especially on those late nights-slash-early mornings.

SHAY MITCHELL

NINE MONTHS OLD

293

Mummy's night off

One American survey found that the average mother spends 98 hours a week on parent-related tasks – roughly two-and-a-half full-time jobs! Mother's Day – the one day of the year designated to celebrate mums – isn't enough, frankly! If you can, devote a regular weeknight to anything that takes your fancy (whether that's relaxing in a foot spa while reading a book or tucking into a Thai takeaway followed by posh chocolates). Just make sure there's only one thing on the agenda: YOU.

294

Becoming a mom to me means you have accepted that for the next 16 years of your life, you will have a sticky purse.

NIA VARDALOS

To sleep train...

If you're considering sleep training (for some, sleep training is a no brainer either way, for others, it requires some thought), only use research methods based on what works for you and your child – not other people's opinions. And if you do go ahead with a sleep training method, it does NOT mean you are lazy or love your child any less, so don't tolerate any sort of suggestion or inference that says otherwise. Ultimately, it's your choice to make.

...Or not

If you choose against sleep training your child, again, this is your decision to make. Similarly, it does NOT mean that you're parenting ineffectively. You're simply doing what you feel is right for you and your baby. You're not expected to entertain someone else's judgment on the matter.

When I had my children, it made me understand that there was a purity to love. That there is an unconditional love.

JENNIFER LOPEZ

Branded babies

It's hard not to coo at the sight of a cute baby all suited and booted for a wedding or sporting an adorable novelty outfit, but this can be an unnecessary expense for one occasion. With or without that teeny-tiny three-piece reindeer jumper, that baby is pretty darn cute!

Wean the wine

The online mum world is littered with "wine mum" memes joking about mothers drawing salvation from a glass of vino post Witching Hour. While it's never helpful to get overly sanctimonious about parents sensibly enjoying an alcoholic drink, it's evident that there's an increasing culture around normalizing binge drinking as a means of self-care in motherhood. Alcohol is, in reality, a depressant which, when consumed to excess, can negatively affect your brain chemistry, however relaxing it might make you feel initially. Then there are the other well-documented health risks associated with boozing (high blood pressure, liver damage, heart disease, various cancers, etc.). Check your national guidelines for recommended limits and seek help if you're concerned about your relationship with alcohol.

To be a good parent, you need to take care of yourself so that you can have the physical and emotional energy to take care of your family.

MICHELLE OBAMA

Bulk buy

Most of us keep our eyes peeled for a good buy-one-get-one-free (BOGOF) or generous yellow sticker at the supermarket. But money-saving experts have suggested that it makes far more sense to buy items with significant savings in bulk – especially for new parents when baby-related products are often hugely expensive. We're not talking stockpile! Just buying enough to make the most of those deals and help save costs in the long run.

Storage solutions

Bulk-buying baby items is great for cost-cutting, but less practical in space-saving terms. If counter clutter and crammed cupboards are a concern, think of sourcing things like big baskets, under-the-bed storage and a second-hand chest freezer for frozen bulk food buys. You may even find that local charities, either in-store or online, are offering pre-owned homeware for free.

Get a slow cooker

If you haven't already done so, then consider treating yourself to a slow cooker. It's a total game changer for time-pressured new mums wanting a nutritious, tasty meal for dinner. Some slow-cooker recipes bypass preparation entirely (chopping and browning, for example), only requiring you to chuck all the ingredients into the pot, set the cooker and enjoy a faff-free homecooked meal later that day. Purchasing this essential gadget is entirely justified, not least for the extra cuddle time it'll free up for you and baby.

Free childproofing!

Now is typically the time when baby is becoming more mobile, when childproofing the kitchen cupboards is more pressing. Before forking out on costly child locks, try wrapping a hairband in a figure-of-eight shape around your cupboard handles (if positioned side-by-side). Any time you need to access either, simply unhook and replace in the same way as before. It's a great travel tip too, for when you're holidaying in rented accommodation and need an easy means of childproofing – fast.

How are you?

Ask yourself daily: "How am I feeling today?" If you're feeling low, think about ways to lift your mood. Perhaps meeting a friend, some time to yourself or talking to someone professionally could help? See this self-questioning as a means of preventing negative feelings spiralling. It might sound trite, but it is true: a happy mother makes for a happy baby.

Self-soothe with a sob!

Indulging in a good cry can improve wellbeing longer term, however sad you might feel at the time. The feel-good chemicals (oxytocin and endogenous opioids or endorphins) released when you sob can bring a sense of calm, allowing you to process your emotions better. If episodes feel overwhelming and are accompanied by symptoms of depression, do speak to your maternity team – it can make a huge difference.

I have found being a mother has made me emotionally raw in many situations. Your heart is beating outside your body when you have a baby.

KATE BECKINSALE

A little perspective

"There are so many things that used to monopolize my time and my energy that I realize now, in the face of being a mother, are just completely irrelevant," said Debra Messing when she became a mum. And how right she is. Nurturing a small human's every need can be exhausting, but in creating and nourishing that person's existence, you may find the stuff you sweated over before (the late train, the dishes in the sink, the passive-aggressive colleague who drove you up the wall) now falls out of importance. Your gorgeous baby and the unconditional love between you both is all that really matters. And that's something to truly celebrate.

Funny baby!

Nine months is a great age for playing games with your baby. With communication a bit more two-way-street, you can introduce games that'll make you squeal with delight too. Hide-the-toy, peek-a-boo and puppet shows are all great ways of engaging with your baby. And there's nothing sweeter for the soul than sharing a giggle with your chuckling cherub.

Helping others

Helping others (perhaps by volunteering for a charity) has been scientifically proven to benefit our wellbeing, making us feel more connected with our community and less stressed. Helping others may even lengthen our lifespan. As a time-poor new mum, finding a few hours to help others is highly unlikely, but donating outgrown baby clothes to a mother-and-baby cause could be a brilliant way of connecting with others.

I feel more beautiful than I've ever felt because I've given birth. I have never felt like I had such a purpose on this earth.

BEYONCÉ

Restock the fruit bowl

A fruit bowl can be a source of annoyance when the very sight (and smell) of blackened bananas hits you on your way into the kitchen. Yet, we're more likely to pick up a piece of fruit for snacking if it's right in front of us. If you're breastfeeding and your hormones are still playing havoc with your system, stock up on vitamin-C-loaded citrus fruits (and don't throw away those over-ripe bananas – they're great for easing constipation!).

Break for *you*

Lunch break, for many mums starting or returning to work is a massive highlight. It's unsurprising really, given that time enough for toilet breaks let alone sixty minutes to eat something can be a battle on maternity leave! This may feel like a golden opportunity to tick things off that never-ending shopping list, but try to balance the chores with activities for yourself, too. Whether it's lunching with a colleague or perusing a bookshop, taking time out will stop you returning to your desk feeling frazzled and short on energy for the remainder of the day.

Stair care

On days when you're at home with a poorly baby or on the back of a bad night, you might feel in need of a mojo boost. Wearing suitable footwear (so not a big pair of bunny slippers), try walking up and down the stairs until you're a little breathless, but not overexerted.

I've been a waitress, an actress, a princess, a duchess. The most important title I will ever have is "Mom".

MEGHAN MARKLE

TEN MONTHS OLD

(316)

You're not super mum!

Is it a bird? Is it a plane? No, it's a mum who, while utterly brilliant at being a mother, doesn't have supernatural powers. You're a human being and, like every human, have your limits. It doesn't mean you love your child any less, quite the opposite: you love your baby so much, you want to be the best possible mother you can be. For that to happen, take however much time available away from the relentless routine.

(317)

Many moms today feel they have to be super moms. I think it's really important to know when to ask for help.

ELIZABETH BANKS

I would probably go anywhere with my kids that I would go as an adult solo traveller.

PEREZ HILTON

I need a holiday!

There's no denying that holidaying with a baby comes with challenges. A change of scenery could just be what you need, though, especially if your surroundings have started to feel a little suffocating. There are many ways to help ease those difficulties. First and foremost, you need to adopt the right mindset: that people generally understand babies are unpredictable! If your baby screams throughout the flight, gets a bit pukey at passport control or needs a feed by the pool, rolling with it will be infinitely easier, and a decent person, with or without kids, will totally get it.

Travel essentials

Sleep is likely to be the primary concern of a new mum planning a holiday with a baby. True, you might have to accept some disruption, but investing in or borrowing a few travel items (portable blackout blinds, plug-in nightlights, a decent travel cot with a thick mattress, for example) can be holiday gamechangers.

Spare clothes for you

Any mum who's endured an uncomfortable journey wearing wet clothes thanks to a baby's puke, pee or poo will tell you that packing accessible spare clothes for yourself (as well as baby) is good advice! It's good self-care practice to remember your needs in this way, too.

There are no seven wonders of the world in the eyes of a child. There are seven million.

WALT STREIGHTIFF

Oxygen mask

You know the safety advice flight attendants give on planes... that it's important to apply your own oxygen mask before assisting others, particularly young children? Take this on board beyond your travels! It makes total sense, especially for a new mum – how can you be of help to anyone without sufficient strength to do so? Whether you need to eat, bathe or pee before dealing with your baby, meeting your needs is paramount for efficiently meeting theirs.

When you have a child, you want to be a perfect
mother. You feel like you have the absolute
plan to be a perfect mother — and then you
make a mistake, and we all make mistakes.

VIOLA DAVIS

Getaway kid-free

According to one international travel survey, looking forward to a
break brings as much excitement as the holiday itself. Some 56 per
cent of the 17,000 participants said they had their biggest holiday
high immediately after booking a break; 72 per cent said they got
a kick out of researching their destination's hottest spots; and
77 per cent described going away as a wellbeing and happiness
means. It's clear, a change of scenery can provide BIG benefits.
Many psychologists consider taking time away vital for avoiding
burnout, suggesting (for optimum rejuvenation) holidaying
without baby for at least two nights! This might be unfeasible for
some, but if you're raising your child with a partner, remember
baby has two parents, so tell that mum guilt to do one!

Carry on camping

If the great outdoors was your preferred holiday choice pre-baby, there's no reason why you can't still enjoy a camping break now. Just be realistic. If camping wild and amenity-free was your thing before becoming a mum, you might need to rethink your approach given that rolling with your baby's needs can be much harder in the middle of nowhere. Do your research beforehand, sourcing a tent that's practical and, most importantly, easy to assemble – there's nothing quite as stress-inducing as tending to a baby and a tent that requires an engineering degree to construct!

One of the most fun ways to travel that's super easy for parents and kids is glamping!

ELISABETH RÖHM

Festival with baby

Festival fans! Fear not! Fun in music-filled fields can still be enjoyed, even with a baby. The key, as with camping, is to be super-prepared, packing more than what you think you'll need. Remember also to pack a few useful specifics like a clip-on sunshade, rain cover, portable fan and ear defenders.

List for life

Motherhood is all too often chocka with to-do lists. One list worth doing (as a sanity-saving means for travelling with children of any age), though, is an inventory of all the items you could possibly need for baby at any one time. It takes the strain out of realizing at 2 a.m. that you've forgotten the baby paracetamol when a bout of teething strikes. Or unpacking on arrival and – horror of horrors – discovering that the one toy your baby just can't sleep without is still sitting in the cot at home. Store this list somewhere handy (perhaps on your phone or computer) and keep adding to it as your baby's needs change. Remember always to do a final check just before you're about to leave the house – you'll never regret this!

I never travel without allergy tablets, insect repellent, eczema cream for my daughter and Earl Grey tea bags. I can't survive without my daily cup of tea!

LISA FAULKNER

Gender-neutral clothes

Many mums choose gender-neutral clothing and toys for their babies as a means of preventing other people from attributing masculine or feminine stereotypes to their kid. If you want to avoid appearing confrontational when gifted with something like a big blue racing car for your son or a bubble-gum-pink outfit emblazoned with "PRINCESS" for your daughter, simply give thanks for the thought (don't feel obliged to coo over the gift itself) and later discreetly recycle via a charity shop or clothes bank. Hopefully the message will reach people the more they see your baby sporting ungendered clothes and playing with unisex toys.

I'm so glad I had a daughter. I want to teach her that there are no limits.

SERENA WILLIAMS

Baby bff

If your baby seems happy in another baby's company, exploit this! Maybe you and baby bestie's mum could take turns to give each other time out? Just an hour or so doing something like getting a haircut or shopping (for yourself!) could do you both the power of good.

Parenting shifts as your kids shift. The best
thing for me has been throwing any kind of
parenting manual out of the window.

KATE HUDSON

Stranger anxiety

By now, your baby is likely happy around some people more
than others. Parents take top billing (Mummy, obviously, in pole
position!) followed closely by the loving relatives and friends
around your baby the most. As stranger anxiety intensifies,
particularly around this age, baby can appear to take quite an
exception to an outsider. As mum, you may feel duty-bound to
apologize for your tot's dishing out of daggers and protesting yells,
but in truth, there's no need to be sorry at all. It's not personal. It's
driven entirely by a baby's self-preservation instinct, and anyone
with any sense will understand this.

**Being a mother is probably the hardest
job in the world. I feel like, in a lot of ways,
children come into the world to teach us.**

MARIAH CAREY

Off-schedule days

There will be low-energy days when that evening's dinner is a dubious ready meal. There will be times when you're running so late for appointments, baby groups and commutes to work, there's barely time to brush your teeth. There will be occasions when the most self-care you can muster is mindless channel-hopping while eating spaghetti hoops straight from the can. So what? Your self-care intentions won't veer off course because of a bad day – or even a difficult week. So, don't berate yourself for "off-schedule" days. View self-care, a bit like you would a TV, as a standard service that'll resume after a pause in transmission.

Write on your mirror in lipstick:
"I had a baby. I'm a superhero."

KELLY ROWLAND

Your bond is *big!*

Work looming on the horizon? You, like many new mothers, might be worrying about the impact it'll have on your bond with baby. However, your face, voice, smell and touch will always mean everything to your little one. Yes, your baby is likely to form a close attachment to the caregiver in your absence (and that's a good thing), but you'll always be number one. If you're worried about going back to work too abruptly, perhaps ask your employer about a phased return to allow both you and your baby to adjust. Rest assured, the bond you and your baby have is second to none.

A mother is willing and capable of doing anything for her children.

SALMA HAYEK

A mother's love

Research suggests that a toddler's eagerness to explore stems from feelings of security. They've established so much trust in you, they feel ready for adventure! Remember this a) when you're chasing after your toddler in the supermarket, and b) whenever you question your bond with baby. Never underestimate the power of your relationship.

ELEVEN
MONTHS OLD

Say your name!

How many times have you introduced yourself in relation to your child? It's inevitable, in certain circumstances, you'll present yourself as "mum", but don't lose sight of YOU!

Motherhood is without a doubt something to be enormously proud of. Solely defining yourself as a mum can be stifling, though, and can make your world feel very small. Greeting people with your name doesn't mean you love your children less.

Get rid of the guilt. When you're at one place, don't feel bad that you're not at work; when you're at work, don't feel bad that you're not at home.

KATIE COURIC

344

Temper tantrum

Ask any mum who's raised a toddler about some of the most bizarre tantrum moments they've experienced and the list is likely to be endless. Anything can prompt a meltdown of epic proportions, from being presented with the wrong spoon for their porridge to objecting that cats can't talk. It's dubbed the "terrible twos", but actually it's a phase that can start as early as one! And while definitely testing, calling it the "terrible twos" seems a little harsh when in truth, it's just a child feeling overwhelmed by the range of new emotions they're contending with and struggling to communicate. Your best bet is to find the funny in these situations because a sense of humour will undoubtedly help you cope.

345

I've never met a two-year-old who is terrible. I'm cool with every stage by daughter goes through. I hope she's not looking at me thinking, "Mom, are the terrible thirties coming on with you?"

KATIE HOLMES

The great milk debate

How long you decide to breastfeed your child is your concern. Whether you're moving onto formula, continuing to breastfeed or planning to introduce whole milk exclusively when your baby turns one, no one else has the right to judge! Try to let uninvited opinion on the matter become white noise, repeating in your head: "You can't change people, only your reaction to them."

Power walking!

If your baby starts walking soon (and remember, milestones are not something to be slaves to), prepare to move quickly! At times you might feel like the coyote in *The Roadrunner* as you struggle to keep up. It's challenging, but so lovely to see the joy their insatiable curiosity brings. Stock up on energy-packed foods, hydrate and limber up! Life is about to get very active.

My stomach, even though it will never be flat again, it's still my favourite because it reminds me of my greatest achievement: my babies.

ISLA FISHER

(349)

I used to think, "What if there's an interesting movie and it conflicts with the boys going to a new school for the first time?" Well, I didn't anticipate that was going to be about a two-second dilemma.

JODIE FOSTER

(350)

Lunch power

Legging it to a sandwich shop in your lunch hour can be an easy way of eating when you're working outside the all-consuming job of motherhood. But even "healthy" options sold by sandwich chains can be packed with salt, fat and hidden sugar – the sort of food that does absolutely nothing for your energy and concentration levels. Instead, give your brain a boost with foods like blueberries, broccoli, raw nuts, pumpkin seeds, turmeric and fatty fish (such as tuna and sardines). For a really quick, nutritious and delicious lunch, why not flake some tinned sardines on a bed of pasta with a sprinkling of pine nuts, cheese and black pepper? Fancy dessert? Here's the good news: chocolate is on that brain-boosting list (just make sure it's 70 per cent dark).

First birthday

It can be tempting to plan a first birthday party of celebrity proportions, but remember your baby is one! A cheap madeira from the supermarket will probably be consumed with the same gusto as a handmade, seven-tier, ganache-finished birthday cake. The epic guest list will no doubt mean nothing to a kid more interested in a balloon or plucking the elastic on a party hat. And an expensive toy is almost certainly going to be discarded in favour of the packaging it came in.

Now my children prevail. It doesn't mean my career is less important; I just have to position things differently.

FAITH HILL

Batch cooking

Whether you're back at work or baby is now eating meals more like your own, now is a good time to master the art of batch cooking stews, bolognaises, curries – whatever family favourites work best. It'll save time and money, and bring you a little sanity when dinner on those particularly busy days is already covered. Just cook double the amount and freeze the leftovers.

**All moms are not created equal,
and all moms do not enjoy every aspect
of parenting. Resources, privilege,
race, region, and support all play a role
in how we experience parenting.**

GABRIELLE UNION

Flexible working

Many new mothers thinking about work will be considering flexible working arrangements around childcare. Remember you're entitled to have your request taken seriously and responded to in a reasonable way – and this includes the time it takes for your employer to come back to you with a decision. If your request is refused, they'll be required to justify this. A good employer should recognize that serious issues like sex discrimination and the gender pay gap cannot be addressed if new mums do not feel listened to or valued. If you feel you've been discriminated against, source a reputable free organization specific to your country of residence to identify your rights. It's totally unacceptable for new mothers to face discrimination in the workplace, but if this is your experience, you deserve to be thoroughly supported.

Be your own BFF

Naptimes might now be less stressful, perhaps bath times don't involve full-on breakdowns anymore and maybe a routine is established... But do you praise yourself for such parenting successes? Or do you berate yourself when things don't go to plan? For self-care to prosper, particularly as a new mum, a loving relationship with yourself is essential. Talk kindly to yourself like a best friend would, reminding yourself that, actually, regardless of what's going on, you rock and your baby is lucky to have you.

Like so many working mothers, I feel the constant struggle to be the best mother I can, whilst setting a good example to my children to work hard.

VICTORIA BECKHAM

Back-up!

It's a good idea to have back-up childcare when you're returning to work. Ask someone close to you whether they'd mind stepping in if your caregiver needs to cancel or your baby falls ill. Also check whether they'd mind being contacted by your usual caregiver in the event you can't be reached. It really helps when you feel like you've covered all bases.

Super nanny

Sourcing professional childcare can feel like a minefield, with costs, location, recommendations and compatibility with your child's personality all factoring in what can become quite an emotional decision. It can help to narrow down and visit the registered places that check as many boxes as possible for you, evaluating your and your baby's feelings after visiting each one. Sometimes, a bit like house hunting or meeting a partner, it's an instinctive decision that makes everything fall into place.

Settling in

If you're uncomfortable with your chosen childcare provider's settling in plans or struggling to work around some of it, don't be afraid to ask for some changes. It's such an important transition for your baby and you, so you shouldn't feel anxious about asking for help. A good childcare provider will understand this entirely and won't hesitate to reassure you.

It would be nice to recognize that women shouldn't be treated differently because they take time to bring life into this world.

SERENA WILLIAMS

Postnatal yoga

Yoga-loving C-section mums will be pleased to hear that eight weeks marks the time when you can resume some gentle practice. Try this pelvic tilt exercise, great for strengthening your hips, legs and upper and lower back: lie on your back with feet hip-width apart, your arms straight at your sides and palms down. Curl your tailbone under slightly, feeling your spine settle into the floor, which should relieve pressure in your lower back. Repeat gently as often as is comfortable.

Share the load

If you're raising your baby with a partner and working, typical household and kid-related responsibilities – cooking, housework, bath times, bedtimes – all need splitting fairly. Consider how to divvy the responsibility when those inevitable childcare calls come rolling in, too, telling you your baby's a bit poorly. The struggle of the juggle is real! But it most certainly shouldn't all fall to you.

Therapy benefits

Treat self-care a bit like scaffolding – there to support and steady you in your new mum life – not as a therapy substitute. It can have an amazing impact on your mindset. If you're dealing with intense emotions (depression, severe anxiety, any postnatal mental health issue), address these professionally. If you feel you might benefit from talking to someone, make that first step by reaching out to your doctor, a trained counsellor or a reputable local support group. Again, don't be deterred if a course of action doesn't sit comfortably or work for you – something else might, so don't give up trying. What's important is that you don't ignore your needs. You *and* your baby deserve better than that.

I've yet to be on a campus where most women weren't worrying about some aspect of combining marriage, children and a career. I've yet to find one where many men were worrying about the same thing.

GLORIA STEINEM

Conclusion

CONGRATULATIONS! You didn't just "survive" the first year of motherhood – you *thrived*! You deserve to be so proud of yourself. Recovering from childbirth while raising a tiny person who robbed you of sleep and, let's be honest, sometimes sanity? It's not dubbed "the hardest job in the world" for nothing! Seriously, how is it there are not more mothers running the world? As the late, great Betty White once said: "Why do people say 'grow some balls'? Balls are weak and sensitive. If you wanna be tough, grow a vagina! Those things take a pounding." How wise that woman was!

To finish where this book began, it's a lucky child whose mother understands the importance of self-care because motherhood shouldn't feel like a shrine you enter upon giving birth and are then expected to encounter like a maternal martyr in a vow of silence and suffering. If your child grows up to become a parent too, this is the sort of parenting legacy that'll stand them in good stead.

Self-Care for Busy Mums

Zeena Moolla

Hardback

ISBN: 978-1-80007-393-7

Self-care means taking time to look after yourself, and often it can seem like just another task to go on an endless to-do list. Packed with quick tips and creative self-care ideas - and written with mothers in mind - this book will show you how to maximize your well-being in the minimum amount of time.

The Baby Sleep Guide

Stephanie Modell

Paperback

ISBN: 978-1-80007-875-8

This book provides simple and easy techniques to help you establish positive sleep habits early on that will pay dividends in the long term. It guides you through different sleep teaching approaches so you can find a healthy balance that works for you and your baby. *The Baby Sleep Guide* offers clear solutions to ensure a good night's sleep for all.

Have you enjoyed this book?

If so, why not write a review on your favourite website?

If you're interested in finding out more about
our books, find us on Facebook at Summersdale
Publishers, on Twitter at @Summersdale and
on Instagram at @summersdalebooks and get
in touch. We'd love to hear from you!

Thanks very much for buying this Summersdale book.

www.summersdale.com